Pi

Tales from
The Fancy

Foreword

Four years ago I decided to investigate the subject of pigeons and pigeon fancying. I wanted to see if I could exist in this community and learn how to be a pigeon fancier; I wanted a lived experience and I wanted to see if I could read art through my experiences of keeping pigeons. It took weeks to find a club which showed the need to be 'in the know' and the 'undergroundness' of the community. I was immediately excited by this world. Since then I have spent many thousands of hours attending pigeon clubs, pigeon shows, pigeon social events, racing, breeding, training and looking after pigeons. I have attended funerals, birthdays and celebrated the birth of grandchildren. I have explored the collectivity of pigeon fanciers, my individual consciousness and the language of The Fancy.

This level of participation has enabled real and actual insight directly into the world of pigeon fancying and into pigeons themselves. The more I investigate the more fascinated I become.

One evening I was at the pigeon club taking photographs of the proceedings when one pigeon fancier exclaimed, 'I've been coming to this pigeon club for 30 years and no-one has ever taken a photo!' His words started me thinking about how this culture is undocumented, unnoticed and is at threat of dying out and being forgotten forever (many members of the community are older and very few young people are taking up the hobby). Since joining the 'pigeon world' I have been told many wonderful stories, met some real characters and seen many extraordinary sights. So, I began to develop the idea of creating an archive about the history and culture of pigeon fancying in Birmingham. The archive is particularly relevant to the West Midlands because there are more pigeon fanciers in this region than in any other. This perhaps dates back to the Industrial Revolution when people moved from the countryside to Birmingham and wanted to keep a connection with animals and the land; pigeons and dogs were animals that could be kept in the city. Birmingham was also at the forefront of developments in pigeon racing. Its fanciers were amongst the first to use the railway network to transport their pigeons to distant liberation points.

This book shares some of the insights and themes that came up in the 45 interviews we have conducted as part of the Birmingham Pigeon Archive project and is written using primary research methodology. The book is mostly told in the voice of the pigeon fanciers. Interviews were unstructured which enabled natural conversation and interviewers to respond to interviewees. We have made 30 oral history interviews and 15 videos ranging from one to five hours in length and commissioned a play. The interviews cover pigeons and also uncover fascinating social histories. Birmingham Archives and Heritage Service will house the Birmingham Pigeon Archive enabling public access for now and for future generations.

Alexandra Lockett

Pigeon Clubs and Federations

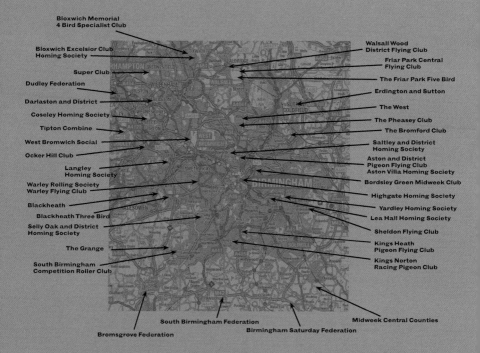

Bloxwich Memorial
4 Bird Specialist Club

Bloxwich Excelsior Club
Homing Society

Super Club

Dudley Federation

Darlaston and District

Coseley Homing Society

Tipton Combine

West Bromwich Social

Ocker Hill Club

Langley
Homing Society

Warley Rolling Society
Warley Flying Club

Blackheath

Blackheath Three Bird

Selly Oak and District
Homing Society

The Grange

South Birmingham
Competition Roller Club

Walsall Wood
District Flying Club

Friar Park Central
Flying Club

The Friar Park Five Bird

Erdington and Sutton

The West

The Pheasey Club

The Bromford Club

Saltley and District
Homing Society

Aston and District
Pigeon Flying Club
Aston Villa Homing Society

Bordsley Green Midweek Club

Highgate Homing Society

Yardley Homing Society

Lea Hall Homing Society

Sheldon Flying Club

Kings Heath
Pigeon Flying Club

Kings Norton
Racing Pigeon Club

Midweek Central Counties

South Birmingham Federation

Birmingham Saturday Federation

Bromsgrove Federation

'...each pigeon club ... belong[s] to a federation and the federation is the body what takes them [the pigeons] to the race point on a Friday night. And they liberate them on a Saturday if the weather's suitable. Then each club... they're governed by [a federation] ... this is the West Midland region... they're the governing body and all members of the West Midland region have to abide [by their rules]... [Then] there's the RPRA [Royal Pigeon Racing Association] rules, which everybody has to abide by and then if there's any disputes or that sort of thing it comes to the region first. The region committee make a decision and then, if they're not satisfied with that decision then they can appeal to the governing body, which is the RPRA council.

Well, there's thirteen regions. That covers down to the south... down to Devon and Cornwall and up to Cumbria and across to Norfolk and then a little part of Wales. Scotland have got their own union and the Welsh have got theirs but there's just a little bit at the bottom of Wales which comes into the RPRA.

Each year the RPRA have an annual general meeting where people can put rule changes in if they so wish, which have to come from a club to the region and then, if they agree, they pass them onto the council. But you more or less... you have to abide by those rules. Each club has their own domestic rules, which cover when you go to the club for marking and clock setting, prizes and subscriptions. All them sort of things are like domestic rules but then you have the basic RPRA rules for what sort of clocks you can use and the conditions that you time in on have to be covered by different rules.'

Ann Edwards

'I do clock setting for the Aston Flying Club down in Aston, been doing that for a few years for Fred. Basically on a Friday evening we get all the clocks out of the cupboard and have to set them up for the racing, might not just be T3's, there might be some STB mechanicals, quartz, Benzing clocks and they have to be set with a paper roll, a bit more involved with the setting. But with the T3's they're left running you don't have to stop them and all you have to do with those is open the case, press top button A and put it into time set, close the case and they're ready for racing, then you strike it and it zeros the seconds to the master timer so it should be bang on time to the master when it leaves the club, then you have to put the seals on. Years ago the Hazelwell Flying Club in Stirchley approached me to clock set for them because they were having quite a few problems, they were all mechanical Toulet clocks then, so I went and helped them out with that and I stayed there for quite a long time, nice club and I got on with everyone well.'

Phillip Mills

'You'd get about 20 or 30 blokes competing, some would be flying on Saturday and some on a Sunday. They'd be fighting on a Wednesday, 'cos they held a meeting on Wednesday, "you twisted me, mine did a full turn and you've only given me a half turn." I used to have a note book and write it all down. Ooooh dear, we had some games! It was in Bordesley Green the headquarters, at the Gypsy's Tent pub. But that was it, one or two upset, ya know.

I've always been a clock setter or chairman, I always been something in whatever club I've been in, secretary, I used to be secretary when you had to work out the results by long hand. I used to be up late at night, I was always decent at maths, well it was in my job, being a toolmaker.'

Bernard Hemming

'Everybody's equal, everybody's friends, I get enjoyment out of people, they treat me as a human being, for what I am. I've made a lot of good friends and I've lost a lot of good friends, they've passed away now.'

Joe Murphy

'One of the most famous Birmingham roller men was a man called Penson. He writ [sic] a book. That's the only book I've ever been able to get out of the library about tumbler pigeons. Well, Penson went over to America and developed the Birmingham roller over in America.

And then I was lucky. One Saturday morning... my mate Roy worked in the meat market and right outside the meat market there was a pub called The Drovers Arms. And this Penson comes over from America to go round the country for a month and show people these pigeons that he's developed and they was what they called a parlour roller. You could get one out of the box, put in on the floor, hit its tail and it used to roll along the floor. I got quite friendly with this Penson and I was really into it, like.'

John Haywood

'I miss the social side of it, we used to love the social side, down the Walsall Wood Club on a Saturday night. They used to come from everywhere, we used to know all the results from across the Midlands near enough, they used to have a piano, come in and sing songs.'

Ron Green

Pubs, Working Men's Clubs and Social Clubs

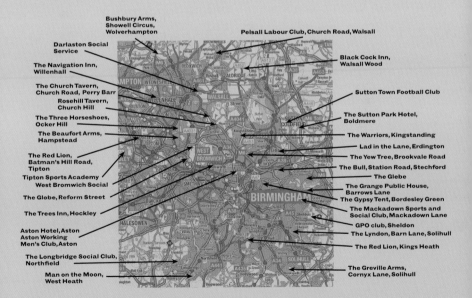

Bushbury Arms, Showell Circus, Wolverhampton

Darlaston Social Service

The Navigation Inn, Willenhall

The Church Tavern, Church Road, Perry Barr

Rosehill Tavern, Church Hill

The Three Horseshoes, Ocker Hill

The Beaufort Arms, Hampstead

The Red Lion, Batman's Hill Road, Tipton

Tipton Sports Academy

West Bromwich Social

The Globe, Reform Street

The Trees Inn, Hockley

Aston Hotel, Aston
Aston Working Men's Club, Aston

The Longbridge Social Club, Northfield

Man on the Moon, West Heath

Pelsall Labour Club, Church Road, Walsall

Black Cock Inn, Walsall Wood

Sutton Town Football Club

The Sutton Park Hotel, Boldmere

The Warriors, Kingstanding

Lad in the Lane, Erdington

The Yew Tree, Brookvale Road

The Bull, Station Road, Stechford

The Glebe

The Grange Public House, Barrows Lane

The Gypsy Tent, Bordesley Green

The Mackadown Sports and Social Club, Mackadown Lane

GPO club, Sheldon

The Lyndon, Barn Lane, Solihull

The Red Lion, Kings Heath

The Greville Arms, Cornyx Lane, Solihull

'Yes, they was in a pub... The Globe, Reform
Street, we used to go there. They marked the
pigeons on a Friday and, obviously, the race was
on the Saturday. I could go upstairs because
the club room was upstairs at The Globe but you
couldn't go in the pub. No, you had to stand
outside. They used to have other meetings there
of other organisations, you know, but I mean
the club room... you could take the kids up to
the club room because, you know... sit there up
the club and a bottle of Vimto and a packet of
Smith's crisps and that was it like, you know.
You daren't say nothing and daren't move.
            Every pub was social. The biggest
thing... I mean, I love pigeons but I love
socialising and, you know, that was what it was.
So, when I was a kid, me and Billy Hassell we
used to go up The Nailer and sit on the wall.
Albert Forester was secretary. I couldn't...
and dad wouldn't join The Nailer. Reason? He
dain't join The Nailer because he don't like
Bank's beer so he went to The Globe which was
Atkinson's so, you know, the only reason he
never went down The Nailer 'cause he don't
like the beers they drink. He never went in
The Nailer. It was rubbish beer. That was its
thing, it was. And it was. Banks's was, until
they [Banks's] went in with Allsopps of Dudley.
It was rubbish beer. You had to have quite a
taste to drink it, you know what I mean. The big
clubs were West Bromwich, The Nailer and The
Globe. There was other clubs. The Wellington
was a strong club and several other clubs had
got good, you know... but the main clubs was The
Nailer and The Globe.'
Bernard Chambers

'Well, I think the trouble is, you see, they haven't got the facilities because somebody comes along, buys a chain of public houses and the first thing they want to do is make it into a young people's social gathering place. So they alter all the pub and you lose, perhaps, your clock room because in lots of pubs you had a clock room and used to mark the pigeons perhaps in the yard, underneath a shed or undercover, where they alter these pubs, make 'em all modern. Well, they don't want you there then, you see. Then, Working Men's Clubs, they've shut because of lack of members and lack of income. I mean, the pub we were at before this one, they've shut it and pulled it down so we're at like a private social club now, where we've got, fortunately, a shed round the back and we're under cover, which is one of the main things... for marking.

I mean, they used to welcome you with open arms and, of course, people could have a drink then which now... you see, lots of them they have, perhaps, a glass of Coke, a glass of orange and then they go back to where they live locally and then they can walk perhaps to wherever they like to have a drink where now you've got to be with somebody else who'll do the driving and, of course, that's a lot to do with it.'

Ann Edwards

11

Birmingham & District Saturday Federation of Flying Clubs

This is to Certify that

Mr _F Prescott_ member of

St Georges Homing Society

took the _Fourteenth_ position in the

Young Bird Weymouth Race

flown on _21st August 1926_ when

_1453_ Birds competed

Distance _133_ miles _313_ yards

Velocity _1229.01_

G J Walford

President

R Berry

Secretary

Bird rung N u RP 26 B#C 842

Birmingham's Favourite Pigeons

THIS IS TO CERTIFY THAT

SECOND PRIZE

was awarded to

Mr. R. Hill

in the SHATLEY & DIST H·S Club Fed:

Race Point SAINTES

Miles 469 yds 655 Birds Competing 221

Ring 77-Z-5641 Colour RED CHEQ

Sex HEN Vel: 1186·49

Date of Race 10TH JULY 1982

G. Evans _____ Pres.

Signed A F Armfield _____ Sec.

Welcome Stranger
Spitfire
The Lady
Young Goliath
Old Blacky
Jock
Mealy Boy
Tracy
Adam Boy
Redditch Rapid
Pretty Polly
Sceptre
Triumph
Repetition
88
The Black Panther
3600
339AVH

(SIRE) Blue N.U.R.P.29A.225 flown Weymouth; he i
1525 Blue Cock flown Nantes, a great winner. Wor
Combine from St. Malo and £60; he is from 503 x 8
Cock flown Nantes, from 1274 x 3458. - 1274 from 1
from 160 x 271. - 8301 Blue Hen kept for stock fro
475 Blue Hen, stock; she is from 269 x 252. - 269
Bournemouth from 503 x 7172, a daughter of G. x H.
Hen flown Bournemouth from 3600 x 7184. - 3600 a s
- 7184 Cheq. Hen flown Jersey from 5630 x 712. - 5
Dawber No.1 pair. - 712 from 504 x 500. - 504 Cheq
to 503. - 500 flown Marennes from 119 x 222. - 119
Bournemouth from 582 x 6869. - 582 Cheq. Cock flov
winner; he is from 172 x 573. - 6869 Cheq. Hen f
daughter of 160 x 271. - 51 bred from a son of 172
Pure Barker Hen bred by A. Fletcher, Liverpool; 1
and Debue I blood. - 222 flown Nantes, a great wi
160 x 271. - 160 from 501 x 58A. - 271 Blue Hen P
combines the strains of Barker's Marica, Irish Gi
Derby II.

(DAM) Blue N.U.R.P.31A.1177, flown Marennes thr
2nd Club, 3rd Fed., 15th Lancs. Combine from Mare:
Club, 3rd Fed., 12th Combine, St. Malo; 1st Club
Combine from Marennes 1935. My 2nd bird from Ma.
is from 58 x 39. - 58 Blue Cock flown Nantes; he
48 Blue Cock from 25 x 475. - 25 Blue Cock a winn
and Nantes; he is from 53 x 677. - 53 Blue Cock :
stage to Marennes including 1st Weymouth, 1st St.
15th Lancs. Combine, 2nd Marennes; he is from 18
Cock son of G. x H. pair. - (7184 above) - 677 Bl
stock from 503 x 8301 (above). 475 see above. -
old Nantes hen, flown Nantes many times, a great
1st Club, 5th Fed. and 35th Lancs. Combine from N
316 x 4. - 316 Blue Cock won 1st Club, 1st Fed.,
from Nantes; he is from 53 x 677. - 4 Blue Hen 1
1st from Weymouth twice; she is from 18 x 475.

36J541.

from 1525 x 475. -
th Lancs.
l. - 503 Blue
x 573. - 3458
G. x H. pair. -
lue Cock flown
air. - 252 Cheq.
of G. x H. pair.
) from 1898 x 12
Cock, own brother
eq. Cock flown
Nantes, a good
51 and a
573, and a
ca, Irish Giant,
; she is from
Barker and
Captain, and

imes, winning
1934; 3rd
t Fed., 3rd
es 1936. She
from 48 x 677. -
rom St. Malo
nner at every
o, 1st Nantes,
184. - 18 Blue
en kept for
lue Hen, my
er, including
s; she is from
Lancs. Combine
ereford twice,

Bill
Breakaway
Spartacus (618)
Jonny
Callum
Conner
Elizabeth
John
Saint-Malo Hen
Squeeker
Jolene
Moody Mealy
Ernie's Choice
Perry Wood
Stephanie
King
Snoopy
Paddy
29
The Black Cock
The Dutchman
707
Sue's Redden
Jimmy
Speckled Jim
Blue James
Jane's Boy
Vincent
Freckles
47

4

Birmingham Pigeon Facts

The first council houses in Birmingham were allowed an eight by five foot loft and eight pairs of pigeons, with an allowance for young birds. The lofts had to be painted green and white – the council colours. The council would come round and put a lead seal on the loft and stamp a number on the loft.

The Birmingham Mail sponsored a pigeon show at Bingley Hall. It was called The Mail Show.

The Pigeon and Poultry Show used to be held at Crystal Palace, it then moved to the National Exhibition Centre in Birmingham. Today the main pigeon shows are in Blackpool, Doncaster and Tipton.

The News of the World used to print the results of pigeon races.

In the 20s and 30s many Birmingham farmers used to keep pigeons.

After WW2, the baskets which had been used to transport carrier pigeons during their service were sold. They sold the two bird baskets (these were used on aircraft) for five shillings (equivalent to 25 pence in today's money) and 15 bird baskets for seven shillings and six pence (37.5 pence in today's money).

The Marriott family bred a blue coloured hen which saved an aircraft crew during WW2. The hen was awarded a Dickin Medal, one of 32 pigeons to be awarded the medal during the war. The Dickin medal is the equivalent of the Victoria Cross, it is awarded to animals for exceptional bravery.

During the war, fanciers could not race their pigeons from France or Belgium and "north road" flying became popular. The birds were released from places in the north of England and Scotland to fly back to Birmingham. There was a north road pigeon club that met at The Bull pub and during the war club membership rose to 100.

There were many pigeon lofts on the allotments on Lifford Lane, Stirchley. Today pigeon lofts on allotments are prohibited in Birmingham but are allowed in some parts of the country, particularly in the north of England.

There used to be several stalls that sold pigeons at Birmingham Markets.

Keeping and competing with Birmingham roller pigeons used to be popular in Birmingham. The pigeons were judged on their ability to do backflips in the air.

In the 1950s Bournville was deemed far too select an area to keep pigeons.

There was no pigeon racing during the first six months of WW2.

Up until the 1960s trains were used to take pigeons to their release point for training and races. In Birmingham the trains left from Snow Hill Station; there was a blue train which went north and a red train which went south. At that time, there were four Federations – Walsall, Dudley and Wolverhampton Federations and the Birmingham Saturday Federation.

Sometimes the buses were so full of pigeons and fanciers going to the railway stations that you couldn't get on them and you had to wait. Often you had to let three or more buses pass before you could get on.

When you went to the railway stations you'd see pigeon baskets on the platforms, waiting to go on to different trains.

In the 1940s Jack Apdale was the gaffer (manager) of the Aston Hotel and kept pigeons at the hotel.

At least one Birmingham couple have found love through pigeons. Their story was told on BBC WM radio on 13th November 2012.

Miler racing was popular in Birmingham. At one time there were over 600 people racing Miler's. Miler's fly in a straight line over a distance of one mile and are timed by stopwatches. However, most fanciers in Birmingham keep their pigeons in their gardens and this makes it difficult to get reliable times since the times were taken and recorded by different people. Usually everyone competing kept their milers on the same allotment or piece of ground. Today there is only one Miler club left in the whole of the UK, in Barnsley.

Pigeon Quizzes were popular in Birmingham. There would be three or four experts on the panel and people would pay £1 to ask a question about pigeon racing. Typically between 50 and 120 people attended a quiz. Most of the money went to charity.

There is park named after pigeons in Central Birmingham – Pigeon Park. It is by Birmingham Cathedral and known as Pigeon Park because of all the feral pigeons that live there.

It wasn't the done thing to keep pigeons in Harborne, it was a 'bit of a posh area.'

Two pigeons (white doves) bred by a Birmingham fancier were given to the Queen as a gift for her Golden Jubilee.

A Birmingham pigeon fancier set up a pigeon loft in Long Lartin Prison. The loft was closed down when there was an outbreak of bird flu.

Local MP Tom Watson wrote lots of letters to the London Olympic Committee to help a Birmingham pigeon fancier arrange a big pigeon release for the opening ceremony of the Olympics in London. Unfortunately it didn't get anywhere.

In Ireland, corn was sold by the half stone (a stone is an old measurement of weight, one stone is about six kilos) in the UK by the peck (an old measurement used for dry materials such a flour or corn one peck is two gallons or nine litres).

There was a pigeon shop on Moseley Road, owned by Harry Hunt, which would exchange pigeons for corn.

The Pheasey Pigeon Club had 40 members. Now only five of the members are still alive.

If you wanted to raise an objection to the results of a race you had to put up 10 shillings (equivalent to £0.50). Today it's £5. This rule is to discourage vexatious objections.

In the 1950s a man originally from Bournemouth used to keep pigeons in a yard in Rea Street, Digbeth. The house was directly behind the Bus Garage and his pigeons would come out of the loft onto the wall of the Bus Garage before flying off.

The Sports Argus paper and The Blues Mail published the pigeon race results.

Even grammar school kids (a few from Waverley Road and King Edwards) kept pigeons.

People used to go and collect orange boxes from the Birmingham Markets to make nest boxes.

During the war the army shot hawks because it was essential that pigeons bringing messages were not killed by the hawks. But now Sparrowhawks are protected birds and they are a major problem for pigeon fanciers in Birmingham and elsewhere.

The Hull brothers had a pigeon loft on side of the railway embankment in Tipton.

Bob Blackburn, sports editor of The Sandwell Mail, reported on local people's pigeon race successes.

The Chinese are very, very impressed with the quality of the pigeons in the Midlands and they have bought quite a few birds. Pigeons from the Midlands and the Black Country have been sent to China and are producing offspring that are winning in China.

During the war people would feed their pigeons bread that had been crushed and baked in the oven. They fortified the bread by putting cod liver oil onto it.

During the war several pigeon fanciers also kept canaries. They used to breed them and sell them to the collieries. Canaries are very sensitive to poor air and the miners used them to warn of escapes of explosive and poisonous gas.

The council built new houses on the Tanhouse Estate in Hamstead. It was a modern estate and pigeons weren't allowed. But Mr Tandy took on the council. He got the unions involved and eventually the council agreed that people could keep pigeons in a twelve by six foot pigeon loft.

After the war, when money was tight, people made pigeon baskets out of banana boxes from the local greengrocers. They used the leather tongues from old boots as hinges.

Most wicker pigeon baskets were made in the workshops for the blind.

There were no female members of the Selly Oak Homing Society in the 60s. Men would bring their wives to the end of year payouts but that was all.

Local boxer Johnny Prescott used to train at the pub where the George's Pigeon Club had their headquarters. During the week the boxing club used the upstairs room at the pub and the pigeon club used it at the weekend. One year Johnny Prescott presented the prizes.

For the end of season prize money payouts the ladies put on their best clothes and all the men wore ties or cravats.

In the 1960s there were nearly four hundred clubs in the West Midlands region. Now there are two hundred and sixty.

In the 1960s the West Midland region had 8,000 members. Today there are 2,000.

Lots of pigeon clubs in the region have lost their headquarters. Working Men's Clubs have closed and public houses have closed so pigeon clubs don't have many places to meet.

If you train your pigeons from Worcester to Birmingham three times a week, over one month it will cost about £280 because of the high petrol costs.

Some pigeon clubs were named after the pub they met in. For example, the headquarters of the Pelsall and District Pigeon Club was at the Pelsall Working Men's Club.

Forest Arts Centre in Walsall ran a course in pigeon fancying, the first one in the country.

Back in the day, it would cost you more if you won a race than lost a race because the winner had to buy beer for all the club members.

**Some of the jobs that the pigeon fanciers
we interviewed do or used to do include:**

Toolmaker
School caretaker
Butcher
Pigeon auctioneer
Electrician
Builder
Mechanic
Roofer
School teacher
Paper boy
Bob-a-jobbing
Apprentice electrician
Gravedigger
Music student
Clock and watch repairer
Pigeon importer
Train driver
Housewife
Tyre maker
Odd jobs
Doorman
Window cleaner
Mechanic
Pet shop owner
Slaughterman
Royal Army Veterinary Corp

Project Diary

10th October 2011
This week I have
spoken to about 25
pigeon fanciers about
interviewing them for
the Birmingham Pigeon
Archive. They were all
very excited! We want to
interview fanciers with
different experiences so
that we get a rounded
view of the hobby – those
who keep Birmingham
roller pigeons, those
who keep racing
pigeons, those who have
official positions in the
pigeon world and the
all important pigeon
fancier's wife!

28th October 2011
Over the last two weeks
I have scanned 825
pigeon race sheets! Fred
Evans, Secretary of
the Aston and District
Pigeon Flying Club, has
kept every single club
race sheet from 1979 to
the present day. It's an
amazing record which,
when looked at as a
whole, highlights many
interesting points. For
instance, one can see
sons who have followed
in their father's footsteps;
how many more fanciers
there were flying
pigeons in the 80s and
90s compared to today;
that many more pigeons
were entered into races
in the past; how the
performance of pigeons
has changed; and that
more pigeons now
come from Belgium and
Holland.

30th October 2011
This week I've met with
several Birmingham
based writers at the
pigeon loft to talk to
them about the radio play
and publication. There
has been a lot of interest,
pigeons can really
capture the imagination.

31st October 2011
Today Project Pigeon was
filmed for The Culture
Show! It was really
exciting, we mentioned
the importance of
pigeon fancying in
Birmingham's history
and culture!

10th November 2011
Today I went to Dennis
Sanders' house. Dennis
had a heart attack 20
years ago and while he
was recovering decided
that he would start
to promote pigeons
and also use them for
charitable activities.
Dennis has done many
many charity events, has
had a pigeon given to
him by the Queen (she
keeps pigeons) and has
been in local and national
newspapers many times.
I took away with me
52 newspaper articles
and photographs of the
Queen to scan for the
archive.

26th November 2011
Fancier Ray Fletcher
and I went to The Racing
Pigeon Show at Telford
International Centre.
It was a great day, Ray
introduced me to lots
of pigeon fanciers I
didn't know and we
recruited a few more
people to interview. I
met three generations
of the Chambers family-
grandfather (Bernard),
father (Dale) and son
(Richard) all of whom
keep pigeons. Richard
Chambers has set up a
pigeon loft in the school
where he teaches. Next
year we're planning to
go and do some on-site
interviewing and video
recording at the show.

11th December 2011
Today BBC West
Midlands came to film
at Project Pigeon's
loft, at Fred Evan's loft
and at young fancier
William Cordon's loft.
We talked about our
experiences of keeping
pigeons, the Birmingham
Pigeon Archive and the
importance of the archive
to Birmingham based
pigeon fanciers and
the wider community.
People's experiences
will be preserved for
the future thanks to the
support Project Pigeon
has received from the
Heritage Lottery Fund.

12th January 2012
This week I put out a
call for volunteers to
help with making the
oral history interviews
and with videoing.
There was a great
response and within a
week we have 15 helpers!
The volunteers come
from a wide range of
ages and backgrounds
and are all very keen!

18th January 2012
Mandy Ross (the writer
we have commissioned to
write some short plays
about pigeon fancying
in Birmingham) and I
went to the local pigeon
pet shop – Jaws, Claws
and Paws in Bordsley
Green. The pet shop
sells pigeons as well as
pigeon supplies. While
we were there we met two
pigeon fanciers, Graham
May and John Haywood.
We spent a good hour
chatting with them.
They are mainly tumbler
men (they keep rolling/
backflipping pigeons) and
told us lots of amazing
stories about their
experiences of keeping
pigeons. Mandy wrote
lots down and I took
their phone numbers
as potential fanciers to
interview – based on our
conversation I thought
that they might be
entertaining! I've passed
their details onto oral
historian Julia Letts
and she has them on her
interviewee list.

23rd January 2012
We went to British
Homing World Show of
the Year in Blackpool
today. It is the biggest
pigeon show in the UK. It
was a great opportunity
to talk to fanciers about
the project and do a bit
of networking as well
as buy a few things that
the Project Pigeon birds
need.

2nd February 2012
Today pigeon fancier
Graham Wilkes, the
writer Mandy Ross,
Reyahn King (Head of
the Heritage Lottery
Fund West Midlands)
and I (representing
Project Pigeon) were
on Carl Chinn's radio
show to talk about the
Birmingham Pigeon
Archive project. We all
had a great time and
discussed the importance
of pigeon keeping in
Birmingham, how the
project is bringing
people from different
backgrounds together,
how it promotes
intergenerational
working and how it is
giving many fanciers
a voice and a place in
history.

4th February 2012
Today 14 volunteers
were trained by the oral
historian Julia Letts.
It was a wonderful
day during which we
learnt a great deal about
interviewing techniques.
Really really excited
about starting the
interviews now!

8th February 2012
Volunteer Sarah Elhassine interviewed fancier Ernest Crozier today. He told some lovely stories about how he started learning about pigeons through keeping tumblers as a boy. He discovered racing pigeons through one of his colleagues at work when he was a teenager and has been racing pigeons ever since. He has even moved house because it is a good location to race pigeons to (good wind, good height etc)!

10th February 2012
Mandy came to pigeon club for the first time tonight. She met lots of pigeon fanciers and really immersed herself into the world of pigeons. She sat in on a special committee meeting where it was decided which new members who had applied to join the club should be admitted. The committee has to decide whether or not the person would be an asset to the club. If they would then they should be voted in.

14th February 2012
Today volunteers Siane Mullings, Graham Wilkes (who is also a pigeon fancier, volunteer and interviewee) and myself went to do an oral history interview with Billy Kitchen. It was amazing. Billy was born in 1915, he has kept pigeons since he was eight and has raced pigeons for 80 years. He spoke about what it was like growing up in Birmingham in the 1920s, about how pigeon fancying has changed, shared his fondest memories of pigeons and much more! We were at his house for five hours and afterwards were thrilled and exhausted!

18th February 2012
Volunteer Sam Owen interviewed her dad today. He was a train driver and one of his jobs was loading pigeons onto the train in the days when pigeons were transported by rail for training and racing. He told a funny story about how once they forgot to load the pigeons onto the train and had to release them from the station.

19th February 2012
Today I interviewed Edna Hunt. It was great to capture a female perspective. Edna comes from a family of pigeon fanciers and although she no longer keeps pigeons herself she is very involved in the 'pigeon world'. She is a committee member on the West Midlands Region and organises coach trips for UK fanciers to Belgium and Holland. I would really like to go on one of her trips, they sound a lot of fun, maybe next year!

21st February 2012
Volunteers Colin, Graham and I went to interview Kenny Briggs. Kenny has been keeping pigeons for a long time and used to keep milers, pigeons that you race for just one mile. There is only one miler club left in the country – in Barnsley. Kenny wins a lot of pigeon races and his neighbour helps him. His neighbour used to have his own pigeons but when he was in hospital his family got rid of the loft and pigeons. As a result he became very depressed but luckily Kenny came to the rescue.

30th February 2012
One of the volunteers, Kate Meng, lives next-door to Ray. Ray used to keep pigeons and Kate remembers them from when she was a child. We interviewed Ray and were surprised to find he went from keeping pigeons to keeping cats! He had to stop keeping pigeons when his wife became very ill and he needed time to look after her.

5th March 2012
Volunteer Graham interviewed young fancier Shane Emmerson. Shane is just 21, he became interested in pigeons when he found an injured feral pigeon on the street. He took the pigeon home, built a hutch and attempted to nurse it back to health but unfortunately it died. He then learnt that there was such a thing as 'pigeon fancying', found some people in his area who kept pigeons and started up.

10th March 2012
Roger Kitchen came to train five volunteers in video skills and video interviewing techniques today. It was a lovely day, we went over to pigeon fancier Ernie Crozier's house to do some practice interviewing and filming at his pigeon loft. We then edited the film and it looks really good. Looking forward to making some more videos!

15th March 2012
Today I made a plan for making the videos. I think it's important to capture the fanciers with their pigeons, something which can't be captured through oral history alone. We also want to document some of the rituals and traditions such as pigeon shows, auctions and pigeon clubs.

17th March 2012
Volunteer Tony Sutera and I went to interview Lynne Adams today. She is the daughter of Jack Adams, a very famous pigeon fancier who had a pigeon called 'Adam Boy' who won The King's Cup in 1968. When Jack died Lynne took over the pigeons. Jack thought that women couldn't race pigeons but Lynne has proved him wrong, winning several National races. When Jack was dying Lynne used to get all the different pigeon corns and take them up to Jack's bedroom and make notes about what was what and which type of corn should be fed to the pigeons when. Lynne feels that her dad would have been proud of how well she has done. Lynne then gave us a tour of her flying-partner's pigeon loft.

20th March 2012
Today I received the first three interviews that oral historian Julia Letts has made – they were absolutely wonderful to listen to!

32

7th April 2012

Ernie and I went to see and film a pigeon liberation in Worcester (at Cob Lane Fisheries). The pigeons were racing back to Liverpool. We arrived at 8:30am and the birds were due to be released at 9am. The weather wasn't too good- rainy and overcast. Luckily there was a cafe at the liberation point so we went and had a cup of tea and some breakfast. The cafe was full of fishermen but we spotted the pigeon liberators immediately- we could tell who the pigeon men were! We went over and had a chat to them and told them about the project and that we wanted to film the release. We had a good chat for about an hour (all pigeons!) and they said they would let us know when they were about to release the birds, they were waiting for a 'break' in the bad weather. They had slept in the van all night. By this point a car boot sale had set up and we had a wander round that. By midday I was getting impatient! We went for another cup of tea and chat with the liberators. They were worried about letting the pigeons go as it was still overcast and they were getting more and more anxious! They were getting loads of phone calls from fanciers wondering when their pigeons were going to be released and the liberators were also calling people across the country to find out what the weather was like in the rest of the UK so that they knew the conditions that the birds would have to fly in. Lots of people were coming over to find out when the pigeons were going to be released so that they could watch, but unfortunately the liberators couldn't give a time. It was lunch time and we were getting hungry so went for another cup of tea and piece of cake. By 2:30pm the weather had improved a bit and it was getting to the point where a decision needed to be made as to whether the pigeons were going to be released today or if they were going to hold the pigeons over and release them the next day. They decided to release the birds, which I was really glad about! And it was well worth the six hour wait, it was exhilarating to see and feel hundreds of pigeons coming out of the baskets. The pigeons flew round and round and then disappeared into the distance.

20th April 2012
Today volunteer Colin
came to video the pigeons
being marked for a race
at the Aston and District
Pigeon Flying Club. This
is the first race for the
club this year and there
was much anticipation in
the air.

24th April 2012
Today I went to interview
pigeon importer and
pigeon race liberator
Jonny Birch. He showed
me one of the most
amazing things I have
seen – a taxidermy
pigeon! I want one!

25th April 2012
Today Ernie and I went to
interview Ronald Green
who owned a very famous
Birmingham pigeon
called 'Breakaway'.
Breakaway won 59 prizes
and over £5000 in prize
money in the 1970s.
There has never been
a pigeon like him. Ron
told us what it was like
having such a pigeon.
Maybe one day Project
Pigeon will be fortunate
enough to have a pigeon
like that!

30th April 2012
Pigeon fancying is
integral to family life
and today I interviewed
a pigeon fancier's wife,
Betty Hemming. It
was good to get her
perspective and to see
how much she helped her
husband with training
and looking after the
birds. The women need
more recognition!

12th May 2012
Tonight Colin came to film the pigeon race results night at Aston and District Pigeon Flying Club. There was the familiar mixture of joy and disappointment in the air. Today fancier Jonny Wynn won. Everyone else was 'going back to the drawing board.' It has been a very hard racing season this year because the weather has been terrible – raining all the time and north east winds which means that the winds are against the pigeons making for hard, slow races.

18th May 2012
Today I finished writing summaries for most of the interviews, the others will be transcribed in full by a professional. Quite tempted to make a couple more interviews! There are a few people that have come up in conversations that sound like they would be good to talk to.

26th May 2012
Writer Mandy Ross and I went to pigeon fancier Joe Murphy's house to see his pigeons return from a race. The birds were released from Newton Abbot at 8:15am, they were released early so as to avoid the heat (a very hot day – the first one this summer!). There was lots of laughing and joking with Joe explaining the ins and outs to Mandy. The pigeons took ages but the sun was out so I didn't mind! All the pigeons came back with muddy feet because they had been down for a drink on a river bank. I videoed the proceedings!

6th June 2012
Today volunteer Hadi and I went to interview John McElwee. Hadi is Iranian and kept pigeons in Iran. He brought his love of pigeons with him to the UK and keeps a few tumblers. It was really interesting for him to compare Iranian pigeon keeping with UK pigeon keeping – very different but the passion is the same! I think I will have to interview Hadi, it would be great to get his perspective. In Iran they don't have racing clubs like here, people usually keep fancy pigeons or Iranian high flyers, these are pigeons which fly really high so they are dots in the sky and stay flying for up to 22 hours! Keeping pigeons is very popular in Iran – it sounds like it is as popular as it was in the UK. Hadi said that sometimes the sky goes black because everyone lets their birds out at the same time!

11th June 2012
I've booked myself a place on Edna's trip to Belgium! Couldn't help myself, I think it will be amazing to go away with a coach full of fanciers and explore the world of pigeons in another country. I will be taking the video camera, I feel a very interesting film for the archive coming on! Now I have to contain my excitement until February.

24th June 2012
We went to an auction held by Wolverhampton Tumbler Club at the Bushbury Arms this afternoon. We took some video and photographs for the archive. It was an amazing afternoon. There were about 120 tumblers, tipplers and fancy pigeons being auctioned by Albert. We met fancier Brian there too; he is a real tumbler man. I was also very excited to see that the landlord of the Bushbury Arms (Keith) has a loft on the pub roof, I really thought that was a thing of the past.

25th June 2012
I went to visit fancier Ray Fletcher today. I haven't seen him since the Telford pigeon show so it was good to catch up with him. I got a surprise when I discovered that he had converted part of his loft into a pub – it's like an artwork! Such a brilliant idea. We drank some Belgium beer. Ray is a real inventor, he has made all kinds of things for pigeons. He made a harness for pigeons which you suspend them in when they have racing injuries such as broken legs or wings. He also made special grills for nest boxes which are comfortable for the pigeons to stand on and make cleaning easier. He has many many pigeon documents which I have taken to copy for the archive, lots of scanning ahead.

9th July 2012
The transcriber emailed, the interviews are hard going because of local dialects and all the different pigeon breeds and names! Luckily I was able to ask a pigeon friend and he helped with the names of the different breeds. The transcriber also said that every time he looks out of the window all he sees is pigeons! I told him that once they're in your mind that's it!

19th July 2012
Mandy came today and we read the first play that she has written. Mandy's writing several short plays, this one is based on a race day. Her other ideas include the relationship between father and son and the role that pigeon fanciers' wives play. Next week she's going to come to results night at Aston and District Pigeon Club to see what that's like.

21st July 2012
The computer and video editing software arrived today, very exciting. Uploaded the many hours of footage that we've already shot and started to read up and brush up on video editing, still a lot to learn!

28th July 2012
Colin and I went to do some videoing with Ray at 'The Black Pearl' (a 'pub' in a pigeon loft!), we talked about and filmed his inventions (grills and harnesses for pigeons), his loft and his pigeons-he has spent a lifetime studying pigeons.

6th August
Chris came to the office today to give a couple of us some extra video editing training. It was a really good day, we learnt a lot and are much better equipped to start editing all the footage that we've been collecting.

8th August 2012
Video editing started in earnest today! Spent about 12 hours editing Ray's interview. It's almost there! This week will be a video editing week.

Volunteers Siane and Colin and I went to fancier Fred's house today to do some videoing. We focused on Fred's role of secretary of the Aston and District Pigeon Flying Club, it's a hard job! We also interviewed his wife Sue, who helps to run the club.

15th September 2012
I drove 96 miles around north Birmingham and the Black Country visiting pubs and Working Men's Clubs that were mentioned by people in the oral history interviews. I took photos for the publication. Pigeon clubs meet in pubs so are an important part of 'pigeon life'. I chatted to lots of punters and landlords who were all interested in the project. One landlady exclaimed 'Oh that was over 20 years ago!' It got her reminiscing. It was interesting to see the locations of the pubs and that they all had large grounds which enabled easy marking and pick up of the pigeons. Next week I'll travel around south Birmingham visiting pubs. I quite like the idea of doing a 'pigeon club pub crawl' and actually having a pint at all the pubs!

11th August 2012
Today volunteer Colin and I went to do some video interviewing with Will Cordon. He's a young fancier who used to help his dad look after the pigeons and when his dad died he took over the birds. We talked about his loft, his pigeons, what it's like being a young person who keeps pigeons, why he likes keeping pigeons and then filmed him and his birds. Our videoing/sound is getting better the more we do.

29th August 2012
The weather is so terrible. Glad that we aren't out videoing today!

3rd September 2012
Volunteer Colin and I went to fancier Graham May's house to do some filming with him. Graham made a lovely oral history recording with Julia and we really wanted to make a short film with him. We met in the morning at Project Pigeon's loft and made a plan about what we wanted to capture. It was a fun day. Graham used to keep racing pigeons but now keeps tumblers (Birmingham rollers). He got his first pigeons when he was eight and he kept them in his grandmother's outside toilet!

18th September 2012
Fancier Ernie and I went
to watch a read through
of Mandy's pigeon plays
at the local pub. It was
really good to hear the
plays being read by
actors, much better than
reading them yourself.
It also gave us the idea
of having the plays
performed at the pigeon
loft as well as recording
them for radio. A play
set at the pigeon loft
would be pretty special!
It could coincide with the
publication and archive
launch. It will be good
to bring all the aspects
of the project together,
perhaps next March/
April when the weather
will hopefully be OK!

1st October 2012
The British Library have
contacted us. They are
going to archive Project
Pigeon's website, so a
copy of the website will
exist forever.

13th October 2012
We've been filming a
pigeon auction by Heart
of England Auctioneers
today. It was a sale of all
white racing pigeons.
They belonged to
someone who had died
and his wife couldn't
look after the pigeons
any more. The pigeon's
names were lovely: White
Emperor, Dark Queen,
The Legend, Shy Girl,
Northern Girl, The Pied
Prince, Destiny, Dark
Angel, Rapido, Sea Lady,
White Splash, Arabian
Knight, Secret Lady,
Wonder Boy, Tranquil
Perfection, Penny Black,
Sea Hawk, Super White
Lady, White Arrow, Lilly,
Mr Tameside, Northern
Light, Valley View Jack
and Miss Flash.

10th November 2012
We went to Doncaster
Pigeon Show today,
my first visit to the
show. It was really
good, there were a lot
of fancy pigeons there.
We met a lot of pigeon
fanciers from the north
of England. One man
was telling us that he
has had his pigeon loft
burnt down three times
by rival pigeon fanciers.
In the north pigeon
lofts are usually kept
on allotments which
makes vandalism easier.
Another man said that
his pigeons fly around
the Angel of the North.
That must be a lovely
sight!

23rd November 2012
This week Project Pigeon
has been on BBC West
Midlands radio, BBC
Midlands Today and
BBC Breakfast! We have
been talking about and
promoting the archive.
It has been a lot of work
arranging it all but great
that there had been a lot
of press interest, fingers
crossed that good things
come from it.

24th November 2012
Colin and I went to
Telford Pigeon Show
today. We did a lot of
videoing and roaming
interviewing. Last year
we went to the show to
recruit pigeon fanciers
for the project. This
year we did a lot of
videoing and roaming
interviewing. We have
come a long way in the
last year.

6

Extracts from Interviews

'One day I went with me mother and she always shopped at the Co-op and outside the Co-op greengrocer's was these orange boxes and mum said, "Look, there's some wood there. You can knock it...." So I started having the orange boxes and then the grocer's next door to the Co-op, they used to have egg boxes and I started knocking them together and I was mekking like little sheds and things in the garden.'
John Haywood

'It was only a matter of feet, the yard we had. The loft was made out of any timber you could get, orange boxes - as oranges came in wooden boxes in those days, banana boxes too. My grandfather used leather belts for the hinges for making the door, it was ok until the hinges wore out.'
Dennis Sanders

'I bought the chassis boxes that the lorries chassis came in, for a pound because it was cheaper to sell them than to ship them back to wherever they came from. I bought two of them and put one on top of the other so they were up in the air and I put sleepers in barrels and concreted them in and put the lofts on top of them so you had to go up a ladder to get to the loft.'
John McElwee

'The pigeons, they used to have an outhouse, next to the brew house there was a built-in coalhouse and the pigeons was kept in the coalhouse, in part of their house, so it was like a two-tier loft as you went in, because you went in and the bottom tier was where the coal was kept. Obviously the coal was kept outside like, you know, and he built a shed to keep the coal and then above it... up in the roof space... he had his young 'uns up there

and his racing pigeons at the bottom.'
Bernard Chambers

'The pigeons used to be on the balcony. I only
had ten pigeons on there. It was all it was big
enough for. It was like a little L shape. It went
along the wall there. I mean the balcony's only
about three foot wide. So three foot that way and
then about four foot that way. So it was only
like a little L shaped one but, once the pigeons
got used to it, it was alright. And it was good
there because I could have 'em out. They'd be on
and off and I could leave them and there was no
worry of cats getting 'em... being on the top like.
        I used to shut it up of a night but then
I did open it most of the day and they'd be on
and off and I'd be sitting out there with them
having a cup of tea and watching them. Me mum
used to say, "Oh them smelly things. Shut that
balcony door." But I used to keep it clean and
it was easy to wash down 'cause it was like a
concrete floor... the balcony... so it was alright.'
Fred Evans

Memorable Pigeons

'I was fortunate enough to have that pigeon
champion "Breakaway" who won 59 first prizes,
plus other prizes, topped the Federation 15
times, he won 20 open races. For two seasons he
was a bad trapper otherwise he would have won 68
1st's & 17 1st Feds. Numerous times when he did
get beat it was by his own loft mates. I was very
lucky to have him. Unfortunately I lost him, he
only had one race left after this one open race
and I was going to retire him. Unfortunately it
was a bad day and he never came back, it was only
from Swainswick 80 odd miles, and he already won

20 from there. You know what they say. Send them
to the world too often and you generally lose
one. It was a sad day, but life goes on.

I've had people come just to look at
Breakaway, I've had them come from Australia,
Belgium, Holland, America, Ireland, Scotland, all
over the place, just to have a look at Breakaway.
If it was an open race, when lots of the members
weren't flying in the clubs, I'd have a garden
full of people waiting for him to come.

My mate bred him, the late Stan Walker.
He was a little checkered pied, as a youngster I
raced him as a hen as he was that small. He was a
pigeon that wouldn't fly with the other pigeons,
he always liked to fly on his own, an hour, hour
and a half on his own, a couple of good feeds and
he'd fly forever on his own. Never seen another
pigeon like him, none can compare to him, he used
to roll [sic] the sky.

I think it was love of home that
motivated him.'
Ron Green

'The best pigeon I ever had was "Old Blacky", he
won for me, 35 prizes in the 1st four when the
Birmingham North Road Club was about 50 or 60
members. He never bred anything although he had
all those wins. I retired him when he was nine
year old, they had a lady's race, well me wife
timed in, she timed in every Saturday and Sunday
'cos I worked Saturday and Sunday, I never had a
day off. She had to clock in and take the clock
in. I said I'd never race him again, he were nine
year old and then on Sunday morning I loosed
them out but he never went out, he stopped on the
front of the perch, I started to scrape out and
he dropped dead on the floor.'
Billy Kitchen

'Connor and Callum, I absolutely loved them,
I loved watching them come, they would swing
round that tree there and just put their wings

back and dive for the house, hit the roof,
straight in the loft, never any trouble getting
them in. They used to race right to the last
minute. I put them in a race, in the Saintes
National, I went to Stratford shopping in the
morning and I worked out they'd be back about
half past two. And when I got back from shopping
it was two o'clock and my friend Graham was stood
outside and he was pacing the floor. "How can
you go out shopping when you've got these birds
coming!" I said "They won't be here yet", and
we opened the house, put the kettle on and went
outside and that's when Connor came round the
corner, hit the roof and went straight in. And
that is when he won the section.

   I loved those boys. They were really
good, they bred nice pigeons, they raced their
heart out. I lost the one in a race and he ended
up in Tyne and Wear, a gentleman rang me up and
said "I've got your bird here, he's going mad to
get out of the loft but it's thick fog up here",
I said, "Well just hold onto him for two days."
He rang me up two day later and said, "I've just
released him", and he was home just after lunch.
I always swore that I wouldn't put both of them
in the same race 'cos i didn't want to lose them,
and I did. I put them both in the same race when
they were five years old and I lost them both.
It was a big race Bugarach, I think it was, a big
national race. And I packed it in at the end of
that year, it upset me so much, it really did.'
Lynne Adams

'One day I come home from school. I was about
five and half and I started messing around in the
garden... in the afternoon when I come home from
school. I looked up and there was a white pigeon
in the guttering, looking over at me like. I run
in the house and I said to me mother, "There's a
lovely, white pigeon" I said, "I wonder if it's
come for my pen." And what it was... it was about
five orange boxes nailed together. Anyway, she
said, "Here, have some of this." And it was pearl

barley. Anyway, I threw some pearl barley in the
yard. It fled down into the yard. Do you think it
would go into this little pen I made? Would it,
well. Anyway, I fed it and it went back up on the
roof and I was worried to death all night about it.'
John Haywood

'I started with pigeons when I was a school boy
aged about 13 or 14. I bought a pair of tumblers
from a pet shop and decided I was going to have
those and build a loft up my garden which I did
do and kept tumblers for a while. It was a hutch
up the garden, I built it on stilts out of little
bits of timber, I just had two tumblers which I
bred which was amazing really. I had me birds
out and because they were new and I'd never had
pigeons before, I couldn't get them back in and
they went on the roof and they were up there
all night. And in those days, being a bit of a
lad, I waited till it got dark and I climbed on
the roof, and went right the way down the roof,
it was a terraced house and so I shined all the
way along the apex of the roof and picked him up
in the dark and got him back home. I wanted my
pigeon back.'
Ernest Crozier

'Oh aye, yeah. It sticks in your head, don't it?
I mean, you have it for a bit and then when you
lose it you think, "Oh no." I mean I had it for
about four years and then I think a cat had it...
next door... because next door's cat come over and I
think it had it... and you're thinking, "Oh God." It
was one of me tumblers that I used to have, one of
me favourite tumblers. It used to come off the roof
and, as it come off the roof, it used to do like a
gambol in the garden and drop onto the pen.'
Fred Evans

'I can still picture now the first pair of
tumblers I ever had, I can still see the first

46

really good kit of competition rollers that
I had, others that stick in my memory are
pigeons that I've been lucky enough to win the
federation with over the years. And also some
of the marvellous breeding pigeons I've had.
One pigeon in particular which was on loan
from a good friend of mine, he was loaned to
me originally because he was getting old and
lost his [nesting] box to a younger pigeon in
his own loft and he bred me a winner right up
to the age of 15, pigeons like that you value.
Obviously there's pigeons that stick in your
memory because they're an unusual colour or
one thing and another. Yes, lots of favourites
over the years, lots. The other thing is, of
course, having always been keen on the breeding
side of pigeons, when you breed exactly what
you want it's a great achievement and a great
satisfaction. With tumblers and tipplers you can
sometimes try for years to breed a particular
pattern of marking or particular colour and
all of a sudden perhaps through years of line
breeding you achieve what you want. It's a huge
thrill basically.'
David Brice

'Where I used to live in Yardley with my mum and
dad I used to see a lot of pigeons flying round
across the road from my house. Little did I know
it was Jimmy Green, who would become my friend
in a year's time. I seen a pigeon in the street
just walking around and it had some nylon or
something wrapped round its feet so I picked it
up, took it off, it didn't seem too healthy so
I took it back and made a little white cage for
it and kept it on the side of the shed till it
looked quite healthy. Then I just chucked it up
but there must have been something wrong with it
because it just came straight back down to the
ground and crashed into the floor.'
Shane Emmerson

47

'He's called Spartacus, it's down to my dad
once again, 'cos me dad saw them as pets not as
racers, if we had a bird that was coming back
really well me dad wouldn't care for that bird.
He would care for the bird that's jumped up on
him and taking corn out of his hand. His number
is 618, we call him number 18, he's a checker
cock and he was always on my dad, he would never
jump on me, it was my dad's pigeon that was. He's
never been a good racer but he's been reliable,
we'd send him and he'd always come back, so me
dad always sent him to keep numbers up.'
Will Cordon

'I had a pigeon and I could tell when he was
going to win, he was a stray that came from
Norwich, I reported it and the bloke wrote to me
and sent a cheque to send the pigeon back, but
I decided to keep it. Of a Friday I'd have him
out and he used to walk up and down the fence, I
thought "you're alright for tomorrow" and he's
won. He's won when he was 10 year old, people
wouldn't believe me, he's won the Channel for me
and his son won the Channel for me.
        I had one and it did laps of honour,
he used to come up the road and fly around and
then go in the pen, it was nicknamed "lap of
honour." The races that pigeon should've won! If
he hadn't have done his laps of honour he'd have
been in the pen and won.'
Joe Murphy

'It was one of those unfortunate situations
when a fox got into the pen and took these two
pigeons and we sent the rings back to the fella
we bought them off. We said we were terribly
sorry, we were really upset about it, the
fox just got in, how, we don't know. The only
thing we could think of was that our door was
a sliding door and if it nuzzled its way in I
don't know. And he very kindly sent us another
pair down and it was one bred out of that couple

that did really well for us. Georgie, on the
Channel he was unstoppable, and he died in the
pen about three or four years ago, 84 pigeon he
was [born in 1984], he won the Heart of England
combine for us, he won me a T3 clock. He was a
smashing bird he was, lovely. You always knew
when he'd come to win, he'd come and land on the
sputnik trap and look at you as if to say "I'm
here" and in he'd go into his box.'
Edna Hunt

'I used to have a pigeon called "Billy", he
would sit on my bike handle bars when I rode to
school, then fly back home. I was the envy of
all the kids.'
Graham May

Family

'Well, we'd had one child, and that was like
alright. It was on a Friday. And then we was
having the second one [child] and I'd sent me
[my] pigeons. Just to try and be sociable, I
only sent four which I thought they'd be the
quickest back. And then I got the phone call
to say the pigeons was up and I was out in the
garden, waiting for the pigeons to come back
and it was almost the time for them to come
back, and I was thinking, "Great" like, and then
all of a sudden she [his wife] come walking out
and she says "Do you know I think I've started."
I just couldn't believe it. I said, "Oh God.
You're going to have to finish then because I
ain't doing nothing till the pigeons have come
back!" Then, when the pigeons come back, I got
'em in. I said, "Well, what do you reckon?" She
said, "I don't know." I said, "Well, I'll go
and take me clock down the club. You'll have

to wait till I've done that." When I took me
clock down the club I done that and come back
and then I said, "Right, you've got my undivided
attention." Then when we've called an ambulance,
because I never had a car, the ambulance was
gonna to pull over on the side of the road. They
reckoned we'd left it too long!'
<u>Fred Evans</u>

'We've always had pigeons in the back garden
ever since I can remember. This house is the
one I was born in. Me brother had tumblers
then years later he had racing pigeons with me
husband when I got married. But me husband had
tumblers at his house too so he was a pigeon
fancier as well. But when we went onto racing
pigeons that's when they partnershipped and they
fled in partnership 'til 1999 when me husband
died, he died sudden. And the pigeons were left
here and I carried on with them on me own but in
partnership with me brother. He had pigeons at
his own house. When me brother passed away my
sister in-law had no interest in looking after
the pigeons so his were sold. And then I kept
mine on here and I raced up until 2010, that was
my last racing season. But I have interest since
then 'cos I'm secretary of a club, a member of
the region and every Saturday I go to my friends
to watch their pigeons.
        Me dad was born in 1905, me mum 1907.
Me dad used to have pigeons, they lived in
Wednesbury town then, in a place called Little
Hill... dad worked in foundries. Me mum said
that dad wanted to know the pigeons were back,
because they lived on a hill in the town she
would put a sheet on the line prop and wave it
in the garden and dad could see that from where
he worked and he would know that the pigeons
were back.'
<u>Edna Hunt</u>

50

'Me dad was me best friend, he used to come
in the lorry with me, when you could have
passengers, you can't now, not really, and we
used to take the pigeons and loose them.
          I've got five brothers and the pigeons
were something special between me and me dad.
'Cos I'd pop home in the lorry, up to mum and
dad's house, and I'd be up the garden with him.
It was special, yeah. I think most fathers and
sons are the same in the pigeon world, they do
tend to be very close.'
Ray Hill

'Disagreements over the way the pigeons were
going to be managed if they were racing, or if
my uncles wanted to get water from the sink for
the pigeons in the days when there was one tap in
the house and someone else wanted a wash, things
like that. Pigeons can become an obsession and a
priority for some people. I remember meeting one
chap who failed to pay his electricity bill and
had his electric cut off 'cos he went out and
bought a kit of pigeons with the money. You can
become obsessional with them, there's no doubt
about that. When you race you see people who
spend money racing a lot of pigeons and you know
the family is going without so they can do that.
Certainly a few years ago you would quite often
see that. Or you'd see people at auctions pay
huge amounts of money for pigeons and the first
thing they do is turn round to their mates and
say, don't tell the missus what I've spent!'
Dave Brice

'Even when I fell in love my first love was the
pigeons. She was my childhood sweetheart, I met
her when I was 12 year old, Susan, I was with her
for 30 odd years, she put up with 'em, ya know,
she knew that my life was set out to be a pigeon
fancier, no matter what was gonna happen I was
gonna be a pigeon fancier through and through.'
John Birch

51

'It was me and me wife. Me and Karen. She always
used to do the paperwork at home and help. And
when I say "we", it's always been a team because
I've always had friends who have helped out doing
the steward's job and putting birds in and out and
all me children, at some stage, have been there
to help. It's pocket money for them. We had six
children and from the eldest down they've all been
involved in it at some stage.'
Mark Evans

          'Well, I'm happy in my situation 'cause I've got
          youngsters by me, you know, to carry on like. You
          know what I mean. Dale (son) and Richard (grandson)
          are probably keener than I was at the time. They're
          looking far... things that I would never do. I mean,
          then again he's got the Internet, which we never
          [had]. How we learnt was talking down the pub: "Old
          Joe's done this, what you been doing, Joe? I tried
          this." You know. And by the time you'd had a few
          pints they let you know what they'd been doing and
          you'd try it. It sometimes worked, it sometimes
          dain't. You educated yourself but today there's
          books and everything.
                      The wife's become a bit left on her
          own, if you know what I mean. Although I try, it
          ain't everybody's cup of tea. Jen's stood it very
          well over the years. She does get involved but,
          obviously, her health now 'er can't get involved,
          you know. But, I mean, it's always been the same,
          always been the same with pigeons. Always knowed
          that I kept pigeons and that was part and parcel of
          pigeon flyer's lives like.'
          Bernard Chambers

'I've just started with my brother, he's got an
old house with a barn, I've set him up, he's never
been interested in them all his life. We hadn't
really mixed, I hadn't seen him for two or three
years then he knocked on me door and said "I want
some pigeons." The last couple of years he's had
odds and sods, some from here and there, we tried

52

to work them but they been no good, so I said
"we'll have some of these Putman pigeons and
fly these." I picked the best out of what we
got, he's just had his first Channel race this
weekend, and he got his pigeon from Massac, 350
miles and he's chuffed to death with that, he
only sent two pigeons. He's got 20 young Putman
pigeons now going absolutely fabulous. His sons
got interested now.'
Ray Fletcher

'Me family comes first, the pigeons come second,
my wife wouldn't agree with that 'cos we've
had a lot of rows over pigeons. Ya know, when
I've worked on a Saturday morning, come home,
"what time the pigeons up, I wanna go out",
then taking the clock on a Saturday night. I've
packed the racing up over that.'
Graham May

'My wife enjoys them, the kids love them, they
want to feed them, it's like a family sport,
it's me and my son, my missus and my two
daughters.'
Mohammed Ayaz

Pigeon Race Day

'It's absolutely glorious to win a race. I'll
start off... young birds, you put them together,
10 days later you've got an egg, 12 days later
you've got another egg, 18 days later you've got
two young'ns, and them little yellow things,
eight days you ring them up, 20 days later to
22 you part them off, you work on them then.
There's nothing like having it from a yellow
thing to a fully grown pigeon and sending it

53

two or three hundred miles and it comes back
and you've done it all yourself, absolutely
fantastic feeling. And to see 'em come its
unbelievable. But it's hard work.'
Kenny Briggs

'My first race was out of this world, people
that don't race pigeons just think "oh it's a
bird flying home", but the adrenaline rush that
you get is more than any other sport you play.
It's like an addictive drug, that drug you get
you can't beat it, when it's in your blood you
can't stop racing pigeons.'
Mohammed Ayaz

'When a pigeon comes home and you've been
waiting for it and you see it coming it's a bit
of an adrenaline rush. The clocking in system
that I use is a manual system so it means that
I actually have to go and catch the pigeon once
it returns home, take the ring off its leg and
put it into the clock. Some systems nowadays
are electronic and it just scans the pigeon's
ring when it arrives home, they don't have to
actually touch the pigeon to clock it in. But
there is an adrenaline rush, you can't get up
there quick enough and get that pigeon in quick
enough because sometimes it's seconds that
count.'
Ernest Crozier

'I got this one particular pigeon, it was a blue
pied. I kept cycling to the cooling stations,
only about 3 mile, and liberating this pigeon
on his own. I did a paper round and put all the
money toward buying a Toulet clock, it was 12
shillings, I give me dad 14 shillings and got
no change, it was all the paper round money I'd
collected. I'd gotta have this race, I'd gotta
race this blue pigeon. The big club at the time
was the Short Heath Flying Club, I asked me

dad, "can you join the club?" He said, "you're
wasting your time, you've got Turner Brothers
and all the big stars", and this pigeon had
only ever been 3 mile. We come 4th in the race.
He was lovely, I can still see the colours and
pigments in his eye. That was 1967, I'd be about
12. I'll never forget that pigeon or that race,
me dad took the clock up thinking we'd be last.'
Ray Fletcher

'The secretary used to ring me at the shop where
I worked and tell me what time the pigeons were
up. He told me what time and then I'd ring home
for Dermot and tell him what time to be at the
loft. This particular day they were over the
Channel. Anyway the secretary phoned up and I
phoned Dermot and I said make sure you're there
at this particular time. Dermot said "are you
coming home?" I said "I might be back." Anyway, I
did come home, I was sitting down and he had the
little table and two chairs out. He said, "I see
you didn't fancy this pigeon and I really fancy
it, I'll bet you a pound that it comes first."
I thought, where is he getting this pound from,
I thought has he been at me pockets? I said to
him, "remember what I've told ya, don't ever bet
with what you haven't got 'cos if I catch you
doing that you'll be in trouble." He said "have"
and put his hand in his pocket and put the pound
out, "you put yours down" he said. So then he
said, "and a time", so I said such a time and he
said he thinks it'll be another time, so that was
another pound bet. I was getting really worried
then, we'd give him pocket money but not a pound,
I thought where's he getting this money from? I
thought that I'd teach him a lesson 'cos I know
I'd win it, well I thought I did, so I put the
money down. He said "do you want a cup of tea?"
I said "alright", he went to the house, made
the tea and brought it back to me. Say he said
3 o'clock, then exactly 3 o'clock a pigeon came
down and into the loft at 3 o'clock, so he picked
up the pound, "I've won that", but I thought has

57

he got the right pigeon? He went down to the loft and came back out and said "I told you that's my pigeon, the one I've marked." I thought that's funny there were two bets at a pound each time and he's won them both. Next thing is the wife come into the garage carrying a little basket that we used to have, she said "have they come back yet?" He'd only sent her across the park with the pigeon and told her what time to let it go. The pigeons weren't even up from the race at all, he'd got the secretary to phone me and tell me they'd been released [they hadn't been released from the race point, his son was playing a joke]. He'd got the money from the wife for doing the bets, she was in on it.'
John McElwee

Pigeon Shows

'I remember going to a pigeon show that was in Bingley Hall, Birmingham. Me dad took me. I'd be about, eight or nine... maybe ten. It was just after the war, I was born in '37 so... And we went over on a Friday. They used to be open on a Friday night then and Saturday and I remember going round. It was all agog to me. The cages really was no different really to today, if you think of the design of the cages. But I mean there was people selling things which I'd never seen before like, you know. It was, I think, roughly half-a-crown, if I remember right, to go in. I don't know if I got in for free or being's I was under... or whatever. We went over. We went on the bus from West Bromwich and he bought a few specifics, like a bit of grit, Kilpatrick's Grit [grit to give to the pigeons] and things which, you know, for the pigeons. You actually just went round to have a look at the pigeons and have a... you know, to talk to his mates. Three or four of us went if I remember and it was an interest to me, a big thing.

I have been to Bingley Hall after that, before I went in the Army like but, I mean, they used to have shows at Bingley Hall. I think there was the Birmingham Show and then after that the Old Comrades took it over I believe. They moved [the pigeon show] to the NEC after which was never the same really. It ain't got the character, I don't think so. But the Bingley Hall shows, I used to like, very much so.'
Bernard Chambers

'I do the shows, I do the Dome at Doncaster, the Old Comrades show which used to be at the NEC, I do Blackpool which is the big show and I do a couple of other shows, I do get a lot of clocks from Blackpool. I do tend to get a lot of clocks from clubs too. When they come up for service I tend to get a lot at once. What some clubs do is they own the clocks and you pay the club say 50p a week for its use and that goes into a fund which is then used to service the clock. After eight or 10 years the batteries do fail.'
Phillip Mills

'We used to do a lot of showing as well, on the shows. I had a great mate Barry Clout who taught me about showing pigeons and the tricks we used to do then for showing pigeons is unbelievable. How to get them right, how to get the bloom on them. Spend a couple of hours a day before, bring 'em in the house, cover 'em in newspaper, warm 'em up and the bloom just came out of 'em. Then you go to the shows. But them blokes are gone now, he died. And there ain't so much showing going on, only at Blackpool, that's the main one or up north. But they don't seem to have the shows round here no more. It's gone completely dead.'
Kenny Briggs

'I used to go to shows at Bingley Hall in town.
It used to be a weekend thing and all the pigeon
flyers used to sit on the balcony upstairs, all
having a drink together and I met one of the
nicest men I've ever met. He was a millionaire
and he was named Sears and Mr. Sears was the
main importer of furs and leather into this
country. I met him at the show there and he used
to show all different types of pigeons and me
and my friend... he's dead and gone... he invited
us to go to his house, which was down on the
River Thames and I've never, I'll tell ya now it
was absolutely marvellous. It was one of these
houses... drive in, drive out... massive house.
When we got there... Peter Brennan, that was
it... who went with me, we had to go to the side
entrance, knock on the door and a maid came to
the door and we couldn't believe it.

Anyway, Mr. Sears come. He invited us
in. We went in and had a cup of coffee and he
said, "Oh, by the way. I'd better tell you. I've
got a loft manager." He said, "I don't actually...
I don't have the time because of business but
I'll take you down and show you."

I'm not kidding you. It was absolutely
immaculate the way he'd done it. He'd built his
lofts in like a square and you went through a
gateway and in the middle was a big lawn. In
the front of every pen there was a sunken bath
for the pigeons to... and he'd got all... I'd never
seen so many different varieties of show pigeons
as what he'd got.

Just show pigeons. That's all he kept...
Mr. Sears. You wouldn't have believed that he
was a millionaire. He was such an ordinary kind
of man. Yeah, down to earth. A proper pigeon
flyer I'd call him.'
John Haywood

'Well, you set up cages and then you invite
people. You advertise that you're gonna have
these shows and you have classes, say flown
classes, so many miles [birds who have flown a

60

particular distance] or just eye sign [a theory
which involves looking at the pigeon's eye to
determine particular qualities] or through the
bars [looking at the pigeons through the cages -
no handling] and then people bring their pigeons
and then you have judges come. You invite judges
and they come and pick which they think is the
best... first three... and then you get, like,
little bits of prize money, and then overall
winner of the show gets... used to get a little
trophy. That used to be out of season and it
used to involve pigeon flyers, because sometimes
now, unless you have a meeting in the winter you
never see... you don't meet socially now. Well,
our club doesn't and lots of other clubs don't
but then, when you have the shows, because the
pigeon flyers come and then you get other pigeon
flyers from other clubs... they come and some
bring pigeons.'
Ann Edwards

'I've been to Blackpool the last three or four
years, it was out of this world. I've been to
the Telford International the past three or
four years, I've been to Doncaster show twice.
Any little pigeon auction that happens I'll go
to. Just to get into that social side of it
too, I enjoy it, it's hard to find somebody
that talks about pigeons or enjoys those type
of conversations, around people that don't know
about pigeons, so when you go to these events
you enjoy it much much more.
        Blackpool is absolutely buzzing with
pigeons and you feel at home. There's a lot of
pigeons there, a lot of stands for pigeon food,
pigeon medicine, pigeon sheds for sale, you meet
a lot of fanciers there, you get to talk to
them, it's a world wide show, it's the biggest
show in Europe. You meet all these people you
read about in the books and on DVDs you buy so
you see all those people and get to talk to them
and you think, I'm meeting a celebrity!'
Mohammed Ayaz

'I used to do a lot of judging, I've judged in
Scotland, Ireland, Wales, London, everywhere
I've judged. I used go on a lot of quizzes where
they ask you questions. I've had to go down the
London Social Circle a few years back and give a
talk on pigeons in front of all the top fanciers
in London. To talk for an hour on pigeons, it
takes some doing. Then I'd have an hour of
answering questions from the audience. That was
nice that was.'
Ron Green

Pigeon Socials

'We've had a good life with pigeons, really, a
very good social life, very good. The payout
at Sutton Town Hall was out of this world, but
all that's gone now. You used to meet up with
your friends. We used to go to pigeon do's and
there was that many there [that] you were like
sardines, you couldn't move on the dance floor,
I think the one down at Sutton Town Hall there
was about 380 and it was a big room, fabulous
that was. We had all sorts of dinners, we had
faggot and peas do's, that was fabulous that
was. They used to come in with their own heater
to keep it warm and we used to have faggots and
peas it was beautiful, then we had the music
and that was absolutely fabulous, really was.
Looking back the times have been absolutely
wonderful. But of course it's not like that now.
And you used to have good pigeon flyers then and
they weren't just good pigeon flyers, they were
friends, real friends.'
Betty Hemming

'Down the George's it was a buffet. They used to
have a bit of a sing-song and a concert and they

used to invite a guest to present the prizes and
they'd have a buffet too. One or two clubs used
to have dinners... a sit-down dinner and that...
but they always used to have a buffet there.

One year they had a boxer to present
prizes... Johnny Prescott, he used to train at the
pub where we used to have the headquarters and
during the week they used to put a boxing ring
up upstairs in the club room. It used to belong
to a group of boxers what trained there and, of
course, some of them got to know him and they
invited him one year to present the prizes.

All the ladies used to go in their best
dresses, their best clothes and all the men used
to wear ties or a cravat, you know.

We have a payout at the club I'm
secretary of now. We have a buffet. One or two
clubs over the country... some of 'em still have a
sit-down meal but that died out round here. You
know, they'd rather come and have a drink and,
perhaps, a sandwich.'
Ann Edwards

'The presentation night was a big thing in them
days, ya know. Ladies got dressed up, you'd have
ya long dress on, the men would have a suit on,
you'd have a nice sit-down meal, it was a big
thing.'
Edna Hunt

Jobs in the Pigeon World

'At about 25 [or] 26 I worked for Birmingham
City Council, I was a plasterer. I met a man,
Dougie Lane, and he first took me to Belgium,
and believe me as soon as I went to Belgium in
them early days, to Lier market, before
any Englishman was there it was like magic,

I couldn't explain to you how magical it was to
go on them trips. We never had any money for a
hotel, we used to sleep in the van or car and fry
any bits of bacon or eggs that we had. We used to
go quarantining, we used to bring Vanhees pigeons
in, what a magical time in my life that was of
going round all them big fanciers that I had only
dreamed of. We met Albert Babbington at the sale
of Marian Meulemans, I was there. Not many people
can say they've held a Dribander, White Nose, a
Kadet. Oh they was fantastic pigeons.

This man, Dougie Lane, said to me "why
don't you come quarantining and do it for a
living?" I said "don't know if I can do it Doug,
what about my wife and kids?" He says "you'll
make enough money, I'll make sure that you make
enough money." I told them all at work that I was
gonna leave and quarantine pigeons and they all
fell on the floor laughing and said "you must be
mad." But I did, I went and done it, the first
couple of years was hard but I soon got into it
and it's been the best years of my life.'
John Birch

'Well, we started getting involved with people
from various countries... and visiting. Selling
pigeons on behalf of famous fanciers from
abroad and bringing a lot of good winners to
this country. You know, getting the gratitude
of people in the UK for quality birds that we'd
imported in... so they could reap the benefits
of having top birds. Well, I would imagine
I've worked with all the main ones. Jos Thoné,
four times world champion. Ron Williamson, in
Ireland, who is probably the best fancier that
there is in the world, in many people's opinion,
mine included. His results are fantastic and
then you've got people like Gaby Vandenabeele
in Belgium. He's a fantastic flyer and very,
very well known. Erik Limbourg, world champion
fancier.

A young Chinese boy kept coming to the
auctions and writing something down. At the

end of one of the auctions I went over to him,
introduced myself and he spoke pretty good
English and he told me he was the son of a
pigeon fancier in China but he was studying at
Birmingham University. So I invited him here to
the shop and he come along and we became good
friends. Then he asked his father and a friend
over to see us and I took them round the lofts in
this vicinity who were successful and he bought a
few birds and he went back and he invited us over
there and did the same for us. Then we've gone
to different shows in China, different lofts and
One Loft races and also manufacturers of plastic
pigeon wares. We imported those in containers
and we sell them here. We're the only ones to be
doing that at the moment.

I've been to Bangkok in Thailand and
pigeon racing is very big there as well. I've
sold pigeons to Kuwait. They're doing well in
Kuwait as well. So, yeah, hopefully in all these
countries we can establish the business.'
Mark Evans

Pigeon Shops and Cages

'There was two that we used to use, they were
corner shops and all they dealt with was
pigeons and corn. There was one down in Aston
called Sterky's, his name was Freddy Sterk but
everyone knew him as Sterky. And there was one
in Hockley, Jimmy Laytham, they used to buy and
sell the pigeons. If I went in Sterky's, he
knew I was after something and I'd say "how much
is that one Fred?" "To you son, to you son...",
that's how he used to speak [Freddy Sterk had
a cleft lip] "To you son. A shilling." Anyone
else would get it for six pence [So, Sterky let
him have the pigeon for one pence less]. Ah
dear, happy days! I used to use them two shops,

three or four of us used to meet down there of a
Friday night and used to go for a drink.'
Bernard Hemming

'The cage I used to go to mainly was in
Parliament Road, Aston. You'd go inside and it
was dark and dusty there was cages on the wall
that had pigeons in probably about 15 inches
square [or] 18 inches square, there were rows
of them on the wall. And he would also have bags
of corn, in them days you didn't buy corn by
the half hundred or hundredweight you'd buy it
by the 7lb or a peck. I'll always remember the
chaps name, Freddy Sterk, and he'd got a harelip
so he talked down his nose, being a kid it was
always a bit funny like. But he was a lovely
old guy and if you was respectful to him he was
respectful to you but if you thought you was
going in there like some did and gonna play up a
bit or pinch a pigeon he'd smack your ear fast
as look at ya. You was always looking, if you
could see a different type of pigeon he knew, he
wasn't no fool I tell ya. And if it was a scrag
it was 2 bob, if it was a good'en it was 3 bob.
Yeah, it was fun.'
Grahame Wilkes

'The person where we used to get our corn from
was in Aston on [the] High Street, just past
the Aston Hippodrome. Although it [corn] was
off ration at that time it was very very scarce
to get the corn and poultry seed, there used
to be a queue a mile long, when everyone knew
that they'd got the seed in. At that time each
shop would only get its quota, once the quota
had gone then it would be another week until
they got more corn. We used to feed the birds on
anything we could get like rice, maize, barley,
even sunflower seed, just to keep them going.'
Dennis Sanders

'There used to be a place... the cage down
Bordesley Green and they used to sell all
tumblers and tipplers. So, when I got me pen
I just used to go down there and buy half a
dozen tumblers and get them flying and then some
more would join your kit and they'd come in and
then you'd breed. Then you slowly built up from
there.'
<u>Fred Evans</u>

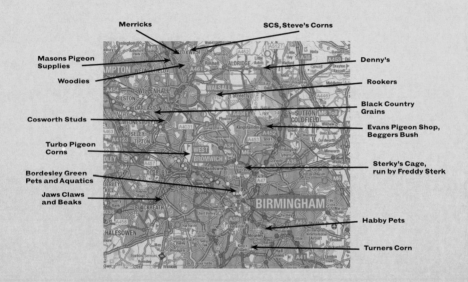

Pigeon Remedies

'A rusty nail, it's supposed to give iron and
phosphate to pigeons and it's just a tonic
but that's what they used to do years ago. If
a pigeon had got what they call a sour crop –
when it's food hadn't digested – and so it's
crop ballooned up and the food wasn't digesting
through, they used to roll... cut a chunk of soap,
roll some soot out the chimney and force it down
the bird's... down its beak then its throat and

67

then hold its beak together for a few minutes
and then let it go and then the pigeons would
be sick and fetch up this sour food back up and
then he'd be ok. He'd always use bicarbonate of
soda, to clear the stomach out, settle it down...
like it'd acid, know what I mean? Then they'd
warm milk to settle them if they'd got worms.
Then, after every race, you always use Epsom
salts. A spoonful of Epsom salts in the water
after a race. It'd break them down, work it
through... all the bad, you know.'
Bernard Chambers

'Donkeys years ago they would give pigeons Epsom
salts, if a young 'un didn't come down for his
grub then they'd have a Beecham's pill, he was
down next morning. I've seen people put woodlice
down their throat if they're being sick. But all
this modern stuff now, and in my opinion only,
it's the cause of losses, young bird sickness
and everything else. Pigeons in some parts of
the country can't even race now without the
support of antibiotics.'
Ray Prescott

'After a couple of years I got to know all the
diseases, when Dutch people, French people
Belgium people sent pigeons, a lot of them in
them early days was full of diseases, full. We
never knew how to treat 'em because we didn't
know about the diseases, but we learnt, we
learnt fast. In this country you could never
get the right drugs at the right time to treat
the pigeons. But in Belgium or Holland you
could get the drugs freely. You used to go to
the vet here with a pigeon and the vet never
ever understood pigeons or knew anything about
pigeons, they knew about dogs, cats, rats, mice
but pigeons was voodoo, they never knew nothing.
But the Belgians had specialised vets in pigeons
and they could treat them, they knew what
paratyphoid was, they knew what paramyxo was,

what one-eye-cold was. They knew the diseases
but we didn't and they treated them, and that's
why their pigeons were superior to ours.'
John Birch

'I invented and I've got the patents today, when
pigeons are in training or racing sometimes they
clip the wires and they break their legs and
it's difficult to set broken legs. You can tape
'em up with what have ya, and god knows what.
I came up with this idea and it was based on an
old sock, cut a hole at the end of the sock,
put his head through suspended him up from his
box and cut two holes for his legs to set. I
said, why not build that in plastic, and I build
this so the pigeon couldn't over eat, he was
suspended just off his box, the leg set perfect
and they could eat and drink at the same time
and that was in all the local press, radios that
was. I never made a penny, it was all done on
trust. I think they still produce the harness.'
Ray Fletcher

'There's more on the market now, there's more
stuff than on the shelves of Halfords I always
say. I used to use Epsom salts on a Sunday to
clear their insides out, TCP in the water,
Johnson's Tonic... that I've used for years, for
iron that is. You could spend pounds on pigeon
stuff, but is it going to do any good? For
canker you used to open their beak and get a
match and wet it and rub the sulphur on.'
Graham May

'There's a lot of talk about drugs they use. I
used to use multi-vitamins, there was a thing
called Aviform which is based on molasses, that
was all I used, they loved it they did, it kept
them fit all year round. There was one guy who
went to Belgium and used to get a tiny little
bottle of this stuff for £60 or £70, and that

was 20 years ago but they used to put it in the
drinker and then there was some they put in the
eyes. It kills it all when you realise they are
using drugs.

One guy was giving them steroids, his
youngsters looked like old birds they were
that built up, but that doesn't always work. I
bought some youngsters of this other guy, he had
some beautiful youngsters, I said to him "will
you sell me some", he said "yeah." I had these
beautiful pigeons. They were as good as I've
ever seen, and I've seen a lot of pigeons over
the years. And they were all dying they was,
dying in the pen, I thought what was going on,
I managed to save one. It was a while afterwards
I found out that to breed these beautiful
youngsters he used to give them turkey pellets
and in turkey feed they use a lot of antibiotics
to make sure, 'cos it's a business, they don't
want their turkeys dying and of course once you
stop them they're not immune to anything.'
Ray Hill

War

'A lot of people used acorns and along the line
there was a bit of a black market in pigeon
corn. If you supplied pigeons to the National
Pigeon Service then you had rations, you got a
pigeon ration book. We used to go to the corner
shop in Beggars Bush, Evan's the shop was.
You supplied young birds and old birds to be
dropped behind the lines in France and places
like that. You sent your best, best pigeons to
fly the Channel, they came back with messages,
you'd take the containers off and take them to
the police station. You didn't know what the
messages said, after the war you found out where
they had been liberated and what kind of message

70

they sent and they issued you a certificate and booklet of all the pigeons that had flown on service work.'
Ray Prescott

Air Craftsman Paul R.A.F. Pigeon Service. Removing message from pigeon after its return to loft.

'During the war they were using them as message carriers, they put a protection order on them and they were shooting hawks so they didn't kill the incoming birds with the messages.

I was five or six, I was in the back yard and I saw this pigeon, it was what you call a red grizzle, I went in and told me dad, it had been a disastrous race from Saint Sebastian, there were no pigeons in three days and that pigeon came on the fourth. The race was over but it was still the only pigeon recorded as returning from that race in the club. And everything that we've got today descends from

that pigeon. That pigeon came from a certain
line that goes directly back to the Dickin
Medal winner, a pigeon called Paddy, he was
the fastest recorded message on D-day in the
Normandy invasion. This one got back and saved
quite a few lives.'
Ray Fletcher

'My granddad was named Clackett. He was a Jewish
man. He was a bookmaker, the only one round by
where he was. He absolutely loved animals. He had
the pony that my mum used to have to take round
the dairy with all the milk on and his pigeons
was his first thing... this is what me mum told me.
        He was a serious pigeon flyer. He was
making money, plus in the 1914-18 war they come
and took all his pigeons off him to use for the
war for messages, to bring messages from France
back to England. He didn't like 'em having his
pigeons, mind you. He tried to hide some of them
because they were his best pigeons.'
John Haywood

The Railways

'Pigeons were transported by railway. The pigeon
fancier would bring his baskets of pigeons
down, we'd weigh 'em, charge 'em, put 'em on
the train, depending on where they were going,
if they were going to Worcester they would
come down about one o'clock, about an hour and
a half to Worcester, and we'd let them up.
And then if it was a summer night they would
sometimes bring them down at 6 o'clock and send
them as far as Bridgenorth, which was say 21
miles, about 6:45 when they got down there and
they'd let them up at Bridgnorth and they'd fly
back. And sometimes, unfortunately, I'd forget

to put them on the train. So what we used to
do, I'd work out what time the train got to
Bridgnorth, worked out roughly how long it would
take them to fly back, and go and release them
from the woods. I've had many a pigeon fancier
come down and talking to his mate "My pigeons
aren't right, they came in this afternoon and
they wouldn't settle on the perch at all, they
were as bright as a button." He thought that
they'd flown from Bridgnorth, but they'd flown
from three miles down the road. We didn't do it
often, it just got me out of trouble.

The funniest thing about it was, the
porter forgot to put the pigeons on so we went
into the woods and let them up. About half past
11, this gentleman came down to get his baskets.
He said "I've got some fantastic pigeons, fresh
as a daisy, they went to Worcester on the
train", he said "They were back in my house
before I got home.' Which was 30 minutes away,
so we had to smooth him off and give him his
money back, he'd realised. If we'd got caught
we'd have been in trouble.

I had another gentleman come down, there
were two pigeons in a box there waiting for him,
someone had picked them up and notified him. He
opened the box and wrung their neck. I said "why
did you do that?" He said that if they can't fly
back then they're no good to him. I thought, why
didn't you tell the bloke at the other end not
to bother to send them back?

There were a load of pigeon fanciers
in Ironbridge at that time. On a Thursday there
was a full train with nothing else but transport
for pigeons, eight to ten coaches, like guard
vans full of baskets of pigeons. And they used
to go down to Frome. I saw how they did them,
they'd stack one pigeon basket on top of another
and get 'em all in rows and they'd put a rope
through the lot so when they dropped the rope
they all come out the same time.'
William Owen

'And then I took 'em to Journey's End, which is
down the bottom... this man was telling me where to
take 'em... which was down the bottom of an 'ill and
they'd got to fly up to get back. Anyway, I took
'em there and then I took 'em to Shirley and then...
he said to me... he said, "If I was you I'd send
them on the train." I said "No, no, no. They won't
get back that easy on a train." And then I rode
all the way from Yardley to Earlswood Lakes. And
loosed them there... at Earlswood Lakes. I loosed
them twice... three times at Earlswood Lakes.

        And I come home from school one day and
me dad said, "I've sent your pigeons." I said, "Ya
what?" He said, "I've sent your pigeons." I said,
"Where you send them to?" He said, "I put 'em
on... the secretary's been down, took your pigeons
for you and he's took 'em to Acocks Green station
and they've gone to Honeybourne." I said, "Ooh,
I won't see no more of them." And, of course, I
got all upset about it. He said, "They'll be back,
they'll be back. Don't worry."

        Anyway, we sat in the garden and we had
about three come back. I mean, I'd only got 15. I
said, "There you go. I've only got three left."
And, lo and behold, about half an hour later I had
17 come back and there was some of this man's. His
youngsters come with mine. Anyway, they went in and
I grabbed hold of them like and I looked at their
wing and they were stamped. His name was on the
wings. So I put 'em in a basket, took 'em round
to his house. He said, "Them are no good." I said,
"Why?" He said, "They've come in to your pen." I
said, "What you gonna do with 'em?" He said, "I'm
gonna kill 'em." I said, "No, you can't kill 'em."
He said, "Do you want 'em?" I said, "Yeah, I'll
have 'em." Anyway, I had these... anyway, I kept on
training 'em.'
John Haywood

        'There were two special trains, one that went
        north one that went south that went from
        Snow Hill. We raced by trains, there were no
        transporters then. There was one called the red

train and one called the blue train, blue was
north, red was south. There was the Walsall
Fed, Dudley Fed, Birmingham Saturday Fed and I
think the Wolverhampton Fed they were the only
Feds going then and they used the trains, and
all the fanciers were there to load them onto
the trains. They would send a telegram and the
gaffer of the pub would put a notice up in the
pub, "birds liberated at such and such a time",
you'd be waiting then.'
Ray Prescott

'Well, them days used to go in West Bromwich
Station, which is in Paradise Street... Great
Western... and you used to go down the station and
you used to go in and they used to have a parcel
room and when you went in there, there'd be ten
or twelve baskets waiting to be collected. So,
when you put your pigeons on, used to go in and
whatever it weighed they pasted it and put it on
the sticker and that's what you deemed [paid]
and so was checked in. Baskets were very rare.
They're dear so you can imagine me dad's basket...
first basket... of course, he couldn't afford to
buy one. He made one out of a Fyffe's banana
basket. That was dad's first basket. It was a
Fyffe's banana basket. Now he had that for two,
I think... well, possible twelve months or two
years but it was a bit heavy. You don't want [a]
heavy basket because your weight cost him.
        What happened one day, we went and I
took the pigeons up and when we got back me dad
lost the basket so dad said he were going to the
station master, you know, because mostly people
knowed one another then and he said, "Well, what
am I going to do?" He said, "I'll tell you what,
Bern" he [the station master] says. "There's
been a basket in there. It's been there now,
gotta be six or eight weeks. Nobody's fetched
it. Have that one." He says, "Anybody comes
along I'll know where it is." So that's how he
got his first pigeon basket... official.'
Bernard Chambers

'I hadn't got a car then but round the corner
was a railway station and I'd take 'em round
there on a Wednesday night and put 'em on the
train to Cheltenham, the station master in them
days used to loose the pigeons ya know, or
somebody who worked on the station like, would
loose ya pigeons the next morning.'
Bernard Hemming

'We used to have the railway, they used to loose
them out on the station, that was another thing
I used to enjoy, going down in the van to New
Street Station round the back in the yard there,
you're talking about loads of clubs, with the
big wicker baskets with shavings in and they
all used to go onto the train then they used to
be released from the train station at the other
end. They move them by road now.'
Graham May

SHOW OFFER £16

£20

£15.50

WITH MENTHOR

AD-HERB AQUA
Water Soluble Oregano
Carr's Natural Improvers

PURIFYING OIL
GARLIC
Carr's Natural Improvers

CLARKS PET PRODUCTS

ETS
TELEPHONE
NUMBER STICKERS
ORDER NOW
ONLY £10 FOR 100
COMPARE OUR PRICE

£8.50

OFF

18/4.50

£5.75

£4.90

Carr's
SUPREME GOLD
PURE WHEATGERM OIL
Carr's Natural Improvers

TURBO BOOST
HEMP OIL
Natural Improvers
250ml
500ml
1000ml

Carr's
NATRAVIT
TOTALLY NATURAL MULTIVITAMIN
Carr's Natural Improvers

Carr's
PURIFYING OIL
GARLIC
Carr's Natural Improvers

Carr's
TRAPPING OIL
ANISEED
Carr's Natural Improvers

S RING STICKERS
FOR £10.00 POST P/D
R 50 FOR £6.00
COLOUR PER 100
RE WING STAMPING USE
RENT COLOURS FOR DIFFERENT
ONS OR FOR COCKS 1 COLOUR
A DIFFERENT COLOUR THESE
ERS ARE WATERPROOF AND LAST
G TIME
WE CAN DO NUMBERS 1-100 FOR
OR 1- 50 FOR £6.00
R NOW WHILE STILL AT THIS

OREGO-STI
A Meriden Animal Health Product

Pigeon

ON SALE HER

7

Writing the
Pigeon Play

Extracts from The Fancy
by Mandy Ross

PART 1: DANCE TO YOUR DADDY

FRANK As a young lad, ooh, I wanted some birds. There was nine pigeon fliers living on our road. But my dad, he worked permanent nights. He didn't like pigeons. I kept on asking him…

Flashback, indoors

DAD I said no, Frank. They're dirty. Rats with wings.

YOUNG FRANK But Dad, they're not dirty, I'll keep them clean. And they're clever. They can find their way home! In the war, they carried messages! They saved lives! Pigeon Paddy brought news of the Normandy invasion. He got the Dickin Medal.

DAD That's as maybe. I said no.

FRANK And that was that. But then one day…

Flashback, out in the back yard

MOM CALLING Frankie?

YOUNG FRANK Shhh! Mom, look, up there on the roof! Look, it's a lovely white pigeon perched up there.

MOM Here, Frankie, a handful of pearl barley, scatter that in the yard, maybe it'll come down for that.

YOUNG FRANK *whistling*
Come on, come on.- *Whispering* – Mom! It's coming!

MOM It is!

End of Flashback

FRANK And it did! It come down for the barley! And then it fled away again, back up onto the roof. It sat there all that day. And then it disappeared.

• • •

JIM   *pause* Look, fighter jets across there, on manoeuvres...

           pause What's that on the roof?

EDDIE   Just a woodie, Jim, don't get excited.

JIM   Come on, where are yous? Call yourselves racing pigeons? Don't let Len's
           get ahead of you... *pause* There ain't a cloud in the sky.

EDDIE   It's beautiful! We'll be getting a suntan. What more d'you want?

JIM   Just a bloody pigeon home – before Len's!

- mobile phone rings –

Is that him? No, phew, it's just the old bird again.

- answers –

Not yet, Maureen. I ain't seen a feather yet, honest to God. I know, I know,
I'll bring you a cup of tea in a minute.

Oh, take my mind off it, Eddie. Tell me about your first pigeons?

• • •

FRANK   *making precise timing announcements –*
Clocks, ladies and gents… And that's… thirty seconds!

JIM   Not a chance today, Eddie. Four hours and fourteen minutes!

DOT   Well, Jim, you never know. Don't count your chickens.

JIM   I'm flying pigeons, not chickens!

LEN   Might be faster if you did, Jim.

JIM   You shut your mouth, Len Jennings. Bloody cheek.

FRANK   Fifteen seconds.

DOT   I heard your birds were early again this week, Len.

LEN   I like to think so!

JIM   *under his breath, bitterly*
Again?

FRANK   Ten.

JIM   Well, we'll see, Len, won't we.

DOT   Shhh.

FRANK   Five – four – three – two – one – UP.

Clocks being struck all around the room.

FRANK   Clocks, please, lads, all your clocks please. Line them up over here.

Sounds of clocks printing out, one after another,
Frank and Dot talking softly in the background
as they deal with the clocks.

JIM   *privately to Eddie*
He's a slippery customer, that Len. Troublemaker. Wish I'd never got him started. He's up to no good, for sure.

My hen my home

My hen my queen my wife my life mother of my chicks
they keep me from you I listen for you I glimpse you
through the wire in the loft in the cage in the sky I
glimpse you in the sky wheeling I hear you I smell you
I long for you I long for you from loft to basket basket
to crate crate to lorry lorry to faraway in my mind's eye
I glimpse you in the loft I think of you I imagine you
faraway I know you I hear you I fly to you

Below me the smell of the sea flowing into estuaries
threads of rivers scents of the cities the ground is
the map below me the sun is the map above me the
wind under my wings you are the map along rivers
motorways over hills fields forest roofs trees streets I fly
to you my hen my queen my wife my life my map my
heart my home

send Heather

Jonny gravedigger (slaughterer) Metal ma

Pigeon themes:

Jo and Ernie *waiting / watching the skies*

2

Pigeon Love
widowhood system, voice of the pigeon
pigeon widows,
women racers, Betty re dances
breeding a champion

Edna   Lyn Adams - Dad not allowed *wouldn't dare* *no washing*
in loft / garden. After he died
Dad

3

Home and away
How do they know where to come home?
Holidays – Graham – the best roads in the world lead to Birmingham
holidays out of season
Fred – not going to his sister's renewal

4

Boys and dads
Graham – I was in the bottom grade of the bottom class. I couldn't write till I was in my thirties. But in the pigeon shed with my dad, it was calm with my dad. And you need to know what the weather's going to be, you need to know your geographics, - I fly the north road, the north east is fairly flat, but the northwest it's rough terrain. Pigeons won't cross the Pennines; they'll fly south round the bottom.

Ernie on the roof
purple pigeon
(lost dads)

microcosm   *men boys*

John Haywood burglary

5

Proud history
WW2
Breakaway,
The Queen

weave in

6

Friday night Saturday morning   *Club*
Striking the clock

Fri night loads of mates
win – no mates

social aspect

Friends all p. fanciers
Sat aft – go to
helping move loft – p. fanciers
if you need help
Or if sick

flashback women getting ready
faggots + peas

gossipy loyalty

Mohammed

click on (actual page)

87

Hanging around . . . and

WELL, fancy that! Is someone confusing their *carrier* pigeons?

In fact, the soft plastic harnesses are a rest cure which has set the racing fraternity in a flutter, if not the birds themselves.

Made by A.V. Tech of Birmingham, they allow injured birds to be supported with their legs free of their own bodyweight while they recuperate in their lofts.

'It will be very useful,' said a spokesman for the Royal Pigeon Racing Association, whose members are among the 30,000 people attending the British Homing World Show Of The Year in Blackpool this weekend. 'Although once a racing pigeon has broken its wing, it only has a small chance of racing again, broken legs can be repaired and this harness will be a great help,' he said.

In the meantime it's just a case of hanging around . . .

Picture: PHILIP DUNN

8

Birmingham Pigeons in the News

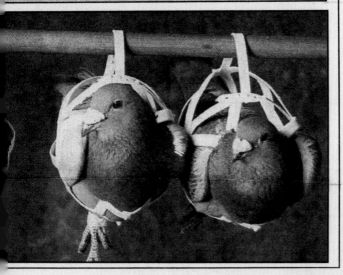

Coup for pigeon fanciers as city archive is launched

Birmingham still boasts more pigeon fanciers than any other UK city – and now an archive charting this historic working class past-time is to be produced for the first time.

The Birmingham Pigeon Archive project has been made possible by a £43,500 grant from the Heritage Lottery Fund (HLF).

City-based Project Pigeon will be working with volunteers of all ages to record the period when competitive pigeon racing began in earnest after the birds' role as message carriers in the First World War. It was a time when pigeon lofts were commonplace in residential streets and thousands of the birds were transported by train around the country ready to race back home. Today there are still hundreds of fanciers in Birmingham keeping thousands of birds between them.

Anne Jenkins, head of the Heritage Lottery Fund West Midlands, said: "This project will chronicle a major aspect of local working class history and will also span generations by giving young people the chance to learn media skills while interviewing their elders."

The project will also cover such local claims to international fame as the breeding of the uniquely acrobatic Birmingham Roller, a type that originated in 1920 in Bordesley Green after local fancier William Penson noticed one of his birds perform a backflip while in flight.

Today there are hundreds of Birmingham Roller clubs around the world and fiercely fought competitions to pick the birds that perform the most dramatic tumbling.

But with pigeon fancying in decline, the

Birmingham can claim to have more pigeon fanciers than any other city

project sets out to document this fascinating part of West Midlands' social history. Interviews with 30 fanciers – including generations from the same families – video footage, photographs, documents and memorabilia will be gathered by volunteers of all ages.

The archive will be deposited at the Birmingham Library Archive and also at Bletchley Park Museum near Milton Keynes which houses an Animals in War exhibit.

The ▶

Project Pigeon director Alexandra Lockett said: "Project Pigeon is excited about working with different communities and generations to document and celebrate the rich culture and heritage of pigeon fancying in the West Midlands. This important archive has been made possible through the support of the Heritage Lottery Fund."

am Pigeon Archive project will chronicle a major aspect of local working class history

Newsdesk: 355 6061, Advertising: Private 355 6901, Trade 355 6161

Betty has a yen to spread her wings

A VIP send off for 'Our Betty' from the Right Honourable Betty Boothroyd MP, pictured with the pigeon's proud Dennis Sanders of Great Barr.

The Rt. Hon. Betty Boothroyd MP was on hand at West Bromwich Town Hall to send off a young pigeon called 'Our Betty', which was named after herself.

This young bird, who is 24 days old, will be one of 20 selected to represent England in a race taking place in Japan.

The pigeon, belonging to Dennis Sanders of Newton Road, Great Barr, will take place in the International Friendship Race in October.

First prize for the leading foreign bird in the 300km race between Matsushima and Tokyo is 500,000 yen.

Any prizes received from the race will be donated to Sandwell Cardiac Club and 114th St Paul's Scout Group in Hamstead, who will be celebrating 50 years of scouting in 1995.

Mr Saunders, who is a member of the West Bromwich Social Flying Club would like to thank I. E. Louella Stud and Stock Nutrition, who have helped him with this project.

92

Left: fancier Fred Evans from Great Barr with his pigeon which will fly in the event.

Patriotic pigeons set to fly high for VJ Day

A SPECTACULAR liberation of 50 red, white and blue pigeons will be a highlight of the Victory in Japan celebration to be staged on Sunday at Perry Barr's Alexander Stadium.

Birmingham County Royal British Legion are arranging the VJ Day Drumhead Service and two minutes silence to remember from 50 years ago the thousands of Allied troops who died in the Far East.

The service at the stadium which starts at 11am, in the presence of dozens of Burma Star veterans, will be conducted by the Bishop of Birmingham, the Right Rev Mark Santer.

Great Barr pigeon-fancier Dennis Sanders, of Newton Road, has been invited to release the 50 pigeons in colour sequence of red, white and blue.

One of the red pigeons he will be liberating belongs to another Great Barr pigeon-fancier, Fred Evans, of Marshall Grove.

Mr Sanders said that in addition to the 50 pigeons will be dark-coloured Queen's pigeon from the Royal Loft at Sandringham.

"It should be a very memorable occasion, with many of the other birds coming from as far afield as Scotland, Wales, London and Maidstone," said Dennis.

He said a special mobile loft was being constructed to transport the pigeons to Alexander Stadium, with Guest Motors of West Bromwich providing a trans-porter to move the loft to the stadium.

Erdington firm, Sign Service, has agreed to support the occasion by writing a smart sign to be placed on the loft.

Flight of fancy

WELLING youngster Jamie Simpson made friends with a former member of royalty last week when he met Stephanie, a four-year-old pigeon.

The bird, once a member of the Queen's own pigeon flock, was introduced to three year old Jamie, of Selwyn Crescent, by its owner Dennis Sanders.

Mr Sanders travelled from his Birmingham home after being told of Jamie's condition by other pigeon fanciers.

He said he hoped Stephanie would act as 'pigeon therapy' for Jamie, who is handicapped with a condition affecting his mobility, speech, learning and hearing and who also has problems feeding.

Mum Sue said it was the first time Jamie had been so close to a bird.

"He was a bit rough with her, but only because he wanted to kiss and pat her like a cat. Afterwards he quacked like a duck. He doesn't know what noise a pigeon makes."

Jamie, suffers from a condition called dyspraxia.

Later this year he is off to America for a revolutionary method of medical treatment which involves swimming with dolphins, following a successful fund-raising campaign which has collected more than £8,000 to pay for the treatment in Florida and travel and accommodation costs.

FANCY THAT: Jamie Simpson meets Dennis Saunders and his Royal pigeon Stephanie.
EC/6097/32

NATIONAL FLYING CLUB

BALANCE SHEET, 25th October, 1947

	£ s. d.	£ s. d.		£ s. d.	£ s. d.
Balance 31st August, 1946 ... ... 3,305 3 5½			OFFICE EQUIPMENT—		
INCOME AND EXPENDITURE ACCOUNT—			As per last Balance Sheet		6 10 0
Surplus for period 1st September, 1946,			BASKETS AND MARKING APPLIANCES—		
to 25th October, 1947 ... ... 1,147 17 3½			As per last Balance Sheet ... 336 1 2		
		4,453 0 9	Additions during period to date ... 21 0 0		
SUNDRY CREDITORS		69 6 0		357 1 2	
PRIZE RESERVE FUND—			Less Sales 10 0 0		
Transferred from Guernsey Prize Money 17 0 0			Less Depreciation ... 26 0 6		
Transferred from Metal Ring Sales ... 339 3 0				36 0 6	
		356 3 0			321 0 8
			STOCK OF RUBBER RINGS		38 0 0
			" CORONATION " GOLD CHALLENGE CUP—		
			At Cost		90 0 0
			Note.—The Club also owns the King George V		
			Challenge Trophy and Continental Challenge		
			Trophy.		
			INVESTMENTS—At cost—		
			£500 2½ per cent. National War Bonds,		
			1949/51 ... ... 500 0 0		
			£1,500 3 per cent. Savings Bonds,		
			1960/70 ... ... 1,500 0 0		
					2,000 0 0
			CASH AT BANK		2,422 19 1
		£4,878 9 9			£4,878 9 9

INCOME AND EXPENDITURE ACCOUNT, 1st September, 1946, to 25th October, 1947

	£ s. d.	£ s. d.		£ s. d.	£ s. d.
To GENERAL RACE EXPENDITURE—			By POOLS RECEIVED		
Convoying Expenses—			Bordeaux Race 1947 ... ... 3,468 4 0		
Bordeaux Race, 1947 659 10 4			Nantes Race 1947 ... ... 3,087 15 6		
Nantes Race, 1947 512 15 8			Guernsey Race 1947 ... ... 1,831 6 0		
Guernsey Race, 1947 294 13 9					8,387 5 6
	1,466 19 9		" ADDITIONAL ENTRIES		
Marking Expenses 180 0 0			Bordeaux Race 1947 ... ... 1,311 0 0		
Clock Setting Expenses ... 320 17 10			Nantes Race 1947 ... ... 1,996 0 0		
Sundries 135 16 1					3,307 0 0
	2,103 13 8		" SUBSCRIPTIONS, INCLUDING N.H.U.		
" SECRETARIAL AND GENERAL EXPENDITURE—			FEES AND CLOCK FEES ... 1,546 0 0		
Advertisements 197 4 0			Less Fees paid to N.H.U. ... 134 7 0		
Printing and Stationery ... 261 0 5½					1,411 13 0
Postages and Telegrams ... 107 18 7			" ENTRANCE FEES		597 9 0
Audit Fee 63 0 0			" PRIZES		
Expenses Allowance—L. Gilbert—			" British Homing World " ... 74 0 0		
Additional, 1946 ... 30 0 0			W. Andrews 5 5 0		
1947 ... ... 359 7 11			J. Banks 5 5 0		
	389 7 11		H. H. Boshier 3 3 0		
General Expenses, including Tele-			R. A. Braithwaite ... 5 5 0		
phone, Telegraphic Address, In-			Alderman T. H. Burton ... 5 5 0		
surance, etc. 128 2 9			Lord Cawley 5 0 0		
		1,146 13 8½	I. J. L. Deaville 3 3 0		
" PRIZES—			A. C. Hall 3 3 0		
Bordeaux Race, 1947—			F. W. S. Hall 3 3 0		
Paid 4,242 1 10			C. J. Harper 3 3 0		
Pool Money not won			S. A. Moon 3 3 0		
repaid, 1947 ... 38 0 3			A. F. Pays 3 3 0		
Ditto, 1946 ... 2 17 3			W. Proctor Smith ... 2 2 0		
	4,282 19 4		P. W. Read 2 2 0		
Nantes Race, 1947—Paid ... 3,327 6 8			A. Ward 3 3 0		
Guernsey Race, 1947—			Capt. F. Worthington ... 4 4 0		
Paid 2,222 5 1					133 12 0
Pool Money not won			" INTEREST (less tax)		
repaid 9 19 6			2½ p.c. National War Bonds 1949/51 6 17 6		
Section G. Prize Money			3 p.c. National War Bonds 1960/70 37 2 6		
not won transferred to					44 0 0
Prize Reserve Fund ... 17 0 0			" METAL RING SALES ... 906 13 0		
	2,249 4 7		Less Cost of Rings ... 67 10 0		
	9,859 10 7		Sum allocated to Prizes		
Bordeaux Race			for Guernsey Race, in		
1946 Cups 33 10 0			accordance with resolu-		
1947 Cups 17 0 0			tion at Special Com-		
	50 0 0		mittee Meeting 11th		
	9,910 0 7		August, 1947 ... ... 500 0 0		
Less Unclaimed Prizes				567 10 0	
1944 1 5 0					339 3 0
1945 1 11 3					
	2 16 3				
	9907 4 4				
Less Guernsey Prize Money paid out					
of Metal Ring Receipts, as per contra	500 0 0				
		9,407 4 4			
" BALANCE OF METAL RING SALES, AS					
PER CONTRA, TRANSFERRED TO PRIZE					
RESERVE FUND, in accordance with					
resolution at Special Committee					
Meeting 11th August, 1947	339 3 0				
" DEPRECIATION OF BASKETS AND					
MARKING APPLIANCES	26 0 6				
" ANNUAL DINNER DEFICIT					
(As per Account herewith)	49 10 0				
" BALANCE, Surplus, carried to Balance					
Sheet	1,147 17 3½				
	£14,220 2 6			£14,220 2 6	

Annual Dinner, 1946

	£ s. d.		£ s. d.
To Cost of Dinner	119 3 0	By Sale of Tickets	107 10 0
" Artistes	25 6 0	" BALANCE, Deficit, carried to Income and Expendi-	
" Menu and Table Cards	4 16 0	ture Account	49 10 0
" Other Expenses, per Secretary ...	7 15 0		
	£157 0 0		£157 0 0

We have prepared the foregoing accounts of the National Flying Club for the period 1st September, 1946, to 25th October, 1947, from the books and vouchers produced to us, and certify such accounts to be in accordance therewith.

REGINA HOUSE,
5 QUEEN STREET, LONDON, E.C.4

6th November, 1947.

(Signed) C. F. BURTON & CO.—Auditors
Chartered Accountants

9

Race Sheets and Official Business

The = King Charles = Homing Society

Old Birds Penzance Race. June 29th 1946
20 Members Sent 94 Birds. Liberated 11-30. Wind S.W.
Master Lost 50 secs.

Member	Bird	In	Velocity	Pools
Hewkin, E.	(R.P.C.RP.44.G.6747	3-34-54	1926	A.B.C.D.
	(HW.44.B.9747			
Cope, G.	(R.C. RP.45.H.8007	3-33-48	1898	Y.N.
	(HW.45.S. 103			
Kemp. J.	B.C. RP.43.D.D.850	3-34-52	1889	B.C.
Gardiner, W.	--------------------	3-35-25	1888	
Scott & Miles.	--------------------	3-35-24	1881	D.
Pritchard & S.	--------------------	3-37-40	1869	
Moore, P.	--------------------	3-38-23	1861	
King, A.	--------------------	3-42-18	1854	
Howell, C. Senr.	--------------------	3-39-39	1850	
Cotterill, J.	--------------------	3-44-36	1801	
Hough & Son	--------------------	3-47-50	1776	
Arblaster, G.	--------------------	3-49-24	1772	
Knott & Son.	--------------------	3-50-44	1731	
Savage, A.	--------------------	3-54-56	1727	
Kidner, H.	--------------------	3-59-18	1693	
Brown, H.	--------------------	4- 3-24	1665	
Fisher, E.	--------------------	4- 4-37	1657	
Feasey, T.	--------------------	4-11-10	1619	
Pinfield, E.	--------------------	4-12-45	1610	
Day, H.	--------------------	4-39-23	1453	

Pools.
91 at 2d.   20 at 1/-d.
40 at 4d.   13 at 1/-d.Y.N.
41 at 6d.   12 at 6d.Spot.

Birds marked for
Penzance, Thursday July 4th,
from 6-0 p.m. until 7-30 p.m..
Will members please
mark Spot and Y.N. on race sheet.
Members are requested
once again to return all Rubber
Rings.
Objections, if any,
in writing within 7 days.

Yours faithfully,

(H. TRACEY.)

Secretary.

Henry Charles H S
Taunton   May 20th 1944   Liberated 12-40 N W

11¼ mins Sent 66 Bds   Markr 4-38 Fast

Prescott & Son	NUHW41 AVH241 B.Ch.	H	3-33-54	966		A
Scott & Miles	NURP42V 9730 D.Ch.	C	3-41-46	930		
A Hoakes	NURP43A 1512 Blue	C	3-47-51	913		BC
W. Windsor			3-50-4	903.3		2° DE
Knott & Holland			3-56-32	878		
A Bottle			4-7-11	834		
Y Feasey			4-11-52	826		
G Read			4-13-6	821		
N Trueman			4-17-34	798		
R Roe			4-26-10	741		
P Moore			5-5-22	680		
H Turton			5-28-24	631		
W Gardener			6-6-32	564		
W Ireland						

POOLS

A 66 @ 2°
B 31 @ 4°
C 95 @ 6°
D 20 @ 1/-
E 4 @ 2/6
Spot 8 @ 6 NOT WON.

Mr Hoakes takes 2° BC + 1° D.E.
with 2nd Pigeon Time 3-50-18 VEL 903.5

Birds race marked Friday next

Gfehr

Any objections to be made with
seven day in writing

W Hatchley Sec.

97

ASTON VILLA HOMING SOCIETY.

Old Birds Templecombe Race.
37 Members sent 293 Birds.

May 24th. 1947.
Liberated 1-10 S.

Master Gained 5 Secs.

S. Fox.	RC	HW.45.	R	7277	1 - 57 - 31	1611	ABCDE
D. Carter.	BCC	HW.45.	W	7524	1 - 58 - 40	1609	BC RS
A. Grinsell.	RCC	RP.46.	HH	1537	1 - 59 - 18	1602	VB RS
H. Thompson.	MC	HW.44.	J	1511	1 - 59 - 13	1601	DE
E. Williams.					2 - 0 - 27	1597	
N. Marlow.					2 - 1 - 17	1590	app RS
O. Owens.					2 - 0 - 55	1588	RS
T. Richmond.					2 - 0 - 28	1585	
E. Heppell.					2 - 1 - 50	1579	
H. Vernon.					2 - 2 - 0	1579	
G. Dayus.					1 - 59 - 6	1575	
W. Harden.					2 - 1 - 53	1569	
W. White.					2 - 1 - 19	1569	
S. Wright.					2 - 1 - 27	1566	
F. Vass.					2 - 3 - 39	1566	
Stanworth & Son.					2 - 2 - 37	1561	
A. Noakes.					2 - 3 - 1	1560	
F. Prescott.					2 - 3 - 30	1559	
C. Stringer.					2 - 1 - 2	1558	
F. Findon.					2 - 2 - 24	1558	
R. Houghton.					2 - 2 - 8	1557	
J. Barker.					2 - 2 - 19	1554	
W. Allan.					2 - 3 - 2	1551	
E. Sigston.					2 - 0 - 56	1548	
O. Bridges.					2 - 2 - 54	1547	
Pritchard & Shorter.					2 - 5 - 6	1541	
F. Smith.					2 - 1 - 50	1540	
G. Reade.					2 - 5 - 12	1536	
H. Tracey.					2 - 6 - 15	1529	
H. Cummings.					2 - 3 - 4	1528	
Probert & Tocknell.					2 - 7 - 50	1514	
W. Baker.					2 - 5 - 33	1498	
E. Munn.					2 - 6 - 27	1496	
H. Ford.					2 - 6 - 12	1493	
F. Simpson.					2 - 7 - 43	1492	
Hough & Son.					2 - 11 - 36	1454	
Gibbons & Son.					2 - 16 - 9	1396	

Correction May 10th.

Probert & Tocknell	3 - 12 - 0	767	

Pools.		K.O.	
285 Birds in 2d.		Fox - Prescott	Ford - Thompson.
145 " " 4d.		Allan - Simpson	Stanworth - Vass
119 " " 6d.			
84 " " 1/-		Birds marked for Weymouth Friday May 30th	
40 " " 2/6.		6-0 to 7-30.	
		Victory Bird bred by owner.	

Please note all meetings will be held every Saturday directly the clocks are finished. Be early.

O. Owens wins H. Thompson special.
Please state full ring particulars on Race Sheet.

OBJECTIONS IF ANY, IN WRITING WITHIN SEVEN DAYS.

H. Tracey.

BIRMINGHAM SATURDAY FEDERATION.

Result of Old Bird TAUNTON Race, Flown Saturday May the 20th.1944.
23 Clubs competing with,3423 Birds.Liberated, 12-40mPM.North West Wind.

Western Section.16 Clubs.2355 Birds.

Beddows J.	West Bromwich S.	3.18.59.	1017.	
Bradbury & Wiley.	Bloxwich. H.S.	3;27.25.	1016.	RP.38 ROB 103.
Southwell S.	Smethwick.F.C.	3.18. 1.	1013.	RP.42.H. 6232.
Hathaway.W.	Bloxwich	3.27.54.	1012.	RP.39.PL. 681.
Forrester.H.	West Bromwich.S.	3.19.54.	1011.9.	
Harper.J.	Aldridge.	3.31.40.	1011.	
Simkiss.W.	West Bromwich.D.	3.21.42.	1011.	
Mogg.C.	West Bromwich D.	3.20.30.	1010.	
York H.	West Walsall.	3.25.20.	1004.	
Saunders Bros.	Bloxwich	3.30.10.	1003.	
Portman.H.	Blozwich.	3.30.48.	1000.	
Morris.J.	Selly Oak.	3.14.16.	996.	
Onions & Son.	Bloxwich.	3.22. 8.	994.67	
Walker.A.	Bloxwich.	3.32.12.	994.64.	
Greenfield.R.	Bloxwich.	3.33.20.	985.	
Darby.J.	Aldridge.	3.35.34.	981.7.	

Eastern Section.7 Clubs.1068 Birds.

Hastings.W.	Erdington.	3;26.39.	1003.RP.43.J. 7232.	
Horton.G.	Saltley.	3.24.34.	993.RP.43.U. 4260.	
Vann & Son.	Ideal.	3.23.33.	987.HW.42.A. 2877.	
Hull.T.	Saltley.	3.24.44.	984.	
Dayus.G.	Aston Villa.	3.26.37.	981.	
Clarke.F.	Saltley.	3.25.32.	981.	
Price.H.	Sheldon.	3.34.11.	980.	

Secretaries,Please send Race Result together with Clock Checkings.
In the Last Old Bird PENZANCE Race there will be £10.0.0. presented by
the Racing Pigeon Co.for birds wearing RP rings divided as follows,
Western Section. £6.0.0. 1st,£2. 2nd.£1; and SIX at 10/- each.
Eastern Section, £4.0.0. 1st,£2. 2nd.£1. and Two at 10/- each.
Birds for 2nd Truro to be marked Thursday next.

Subject to correction,
R.Berrey,
Secretary.

West Birmingham Flying Club
President Mr A. Johns

109 Meeting requested by Mr B. Wainman

Dear Committee Member,

Mr B. Wainman has requested that a 109 meeting be called to discuss a problem
which arose regarding his dials for the Young Bird Wincanton race. This
meeting will be held on Sunday 1st September 1985 at 8.00pm at College Arms.

The Case

On Saturday 10th August 1985 Mr Wainmans' clock was struck as normal but
the dial was badly torn. It was noted that the unlocking puncture appeared
before the strike off print. Later the same evening the dial was ruled
out of order and a committee meeting was called for the following Saturday.

At the meeting a similar effect was produced with the same clock. The person
who struck the clock and the clock setter who opened it stated that as far
as they could re-collect the clock had been intact on arrival at the club.
On the evidence available it was decided that the cause of the unlocking
puncture being in the wrong place was that the dial had not been wound on by
the clock setter before attempting to unlock and open the clock; this
being so it was agreed that Mr Wainman be refunded his race fees.
Mr Wainman was not satisfied with this and requested a 109 meeting.

Yours sincerely,

J.J. Prescott

J.J. Prescott (Miss)
Secretary

ASTON VILLA HOMING SOCIETY

"ASTON HOTEL" WITTON

Gentlemen,

The Annual General Meeting will be
held on Saturday, December 8th, at 7.30 p.m.
prompt.

AGENDA

1. Minutes of the last A.G.M.

2. Election of officers.

3. Show for 1946.

4. Open Races for 1946.

5. Mr. H. Brown will move that "All monies
    for Victory Birds be flown for in the
    Young Bird Race and not left to subsequent
    years.   5 prizes up to £50.   1 Additional
    prize for every further £10 subscribed".

6. Mr. Vass will move "Victory Birds be
    purchased at £1 per bird, with a limit
    of 6 birds per Member".

7. Any other business.

                              W.J. GODWIN.
                                28.11.45

Glossary of pigeon terms

Birmingham roller or tumbler:
A breed of pigeon which is used in performance flying; they do backflips in the sky. They were first developed in Birmingham by tram driver William Penson.

Bob: One shilling. Five new pence in today's money.

Cage: A pigeon pet shop, selling pigeons and pigeon products.

Clock/clocking in: When a pigeon returns from a race, the rubber ring the pigeon is marked with is put into the pigeon fancier's clock. The clock records the time the pigeon arrives back to his home. Before the start of each race, all the clocks are set to the same time at the club and at the end of the race fanciers take their clock to the pigeon club and everyone's time is read out to determine the winner. There are several different kinds of clocks, for example T3 or STB.

Cock: A male pigeon.

ETS/Electronic Timing System:
Rather than having a mechanical clock as above, pigeons are clocked in automatically almost like shopping going through the till at the shops.

Fancy pigeon: Pigeons which are bred for their appearance rather than racing or performance ability. There are many hundreds of breeds of fancy pigeons. There are special fancy pigeon competitions.

Federation: Several pigeon clubs make up a Federation. The Federation is responsible for deciding the race points and transporting and releasing the pigeons on race day.

Hen: A female pigeon.

Kit: A group of pigeons flying together.

Liberation: Releasing pigeons for a race.

Loft: A pigeon's home. Known as a loft because historically pigeons would be kept in the loft space of a pigeon fancier's home. The guano was said to help keep the house warm by providing insulation! A loft is sometimes called a pen.

Marking: Pigeons competing in a race are marked with a rubber ring which is attached to their leg. Each ring is stamped with a unique number and when the bird arrives back at its home loft, the ring is taken off and put into the clock, the clock records the time of the pigeon's arrival. The time is used to calculate the bird's average speed over the course.

North road: Races in which the pigeons fly from the north to the south of Britain.

NPA/National Pigeon Association:
The governing body of fancy pigeons in the UK.

Old bird: A pigeon that is over one year old. There are separate races for young birds and old birds.

One loft: A communal loft which houses many hundreds of pigeons belonging to different people. Because you don't need your own pigeon loft, one loft races are open to anyone.

Parlour rollers: A breed of pigeon which doesn't fly but does backflips along the floor. They are 'bowled' along the floor and the winning pigeon is the one which rolls the furthest without stopping. They are popular in the USA but rare in the UK.

Partnership: Two or more pigeon fanciers who look after and race pigeons together.

Payout: An evening at the end of the pigeon racing season when pigeon fanciers receive certificates, trophies and money for races they have performed well in.

Peck: Pigeon corn used to be sold by the peck. A peck is a unit of dry volume equivalent to nine litres of crops such as wheat, peas and beans and 13 litres of crops such as barley, oats and malt.

Pen: A pigeon's home. Also known as a pigeon loft.

Pigeon club: An organisation made up of pigeon fanciers who compete against each other in races. At the club the pigeons are marked for races, collected by the transporter and race results read out. They meet in Working Men's Clubs or pubs. Clubs belong to Federations.

Pigeon fancier: A person who keeps and breeds pigeons.

Pigeon health: Pigeon fanciers are their animals' vet. Keeping them healthy is very important.

Pigeon race: Similar to a horse race but each pigeon races to their home loft so there are many finishing points and the distance each pigeon covers is different depending on the distance from the liberation point to their home loft. As each pigeon flies a different distance, it would be unfair to award the race to the first pigeon home. Instead each bird's speed is calculated (in yards per minute). The pigeon with the highest calculated speed is the winner. On average pigeons can fly at around 60mph!

Pigeon show: Events at which people in the pigeon industry sell pigeon items such as healthcare products, feeders, drinkers, baskets etc. There may also be pigeon auctions and fancy pigeon competitions.

Quarantine: When pigeons were imported to the UK they used to be isolated in a special loft where they were observed and treated for illnesses.

RPRA/Royal Pigeon Racing Association: The main governing body of pigeon racing in the UK.

Race point: A location where pigeons are released/ liberated from. Pigeons return to their home and are released at distances of between 80 miles and 600 miles from their home.

Shilling: Five new pence in today's money.

Squeaker: A very young pigeon (from hatching to four months old).

South road: Races in which the pigeons fly from the south to the north of Britain.

Tippler: A type of pigeon that flies very high in the sky for many hours at a time (the record is 24 hours). These pigeons are particularly popular in Pakistan and there is a breed known as the Pakistani high flyer.

Training: Racing pigeons are athletes and they need to be fit. Pigeon fanciers train their pigeons by putting them in a pigeon basket and driving them miles away and releasing them to fly back.

Trap/trapping: When pigeons return from a race the pigeon fancier must get the pigeon into the loft. This is known as trapping.

Transporter: A vehicle which holds pigeons and takes them to race points. Prior to the 1960s pigeons were transported by train. Today they are transported by road.

Up: Released up into the sky for a race.

Widowhood: A method of racing pigeons which involves allowing the male and female pigeons to pair off (form couples). The couples are then separated and the male pigeon sent off to the race whilst the female stays in the loft. The male pigeons race back to their mates.

Young bird: A pigeon that is under one year old. There are separate races for young and old birds.

Acknowledgements

Project Pigeon wants to thank the following individuals and organisations for supporting the Birmingham Pigeon Archive project.

The Heritage Lottery Fund has enabled this project to happen and made it such a success. Project Pigeon, pigeon fanciers, historians and volunteers are grateful for your support.

It has been amazing to work with so many pigeon fanciers and hear some wonderful, charming and often hilarious stories. Thanks for your interviews.

Birmingham Archives and Heritage Service will house the Birmingham Pigeon Archive and enable it to be accessible for future generations. Thanks to Izzy Mohammed who has helped make this happen.

Thanks to writer Mandy Ross for her work on The Fancy, a series of plays based on material from the archive. And to Kim Charnock from RoguePlay and Jonathan Davidson from Writing West Midlands for their advice and collaboration.

Thanks to Julia Letts who trained our volunteers in oral history interviewing skills and collected some great stories. And to Roger Kitchen who trained volunteers in video skills.

Thanks to all the volunteers who have helped with the project. Colin Thomas who collected video footage. Siane Mullings who interviewed Billy Kitchen for five hours. Sarah Elhassine who made the first interview. Tony Sutera who interviewed the daughter of a famous pigeon fancier. Kate Meng who interviewed her next door neighbour. Hadi Shaker who came to Birmingham from Iran and brought his interest in pigeons with him. Sam Owen who interviewed her father who worked on the railways. Graham Wilkes who contacted and interviewed fanciers and went on Carl Chinn's radio show. Ernie Crozier who advised on the project and contacted and interviewed fanciers. Will Cordon and Fred Evans who let the BBC film at their pigeon lofts. And Christine and Peter Lockett, Cheryl Jones, Annette Naudin and Ian England for Project Pigeon support over the years.

And thanks to pigeons, who have contributed to society throughout history. You have served in the army; been postmen; transported news; given Charles Darwin the clue to help him develop the Theory of Evolution; you have a place in all major religions; and you have inspired artists, musicians, filmmakers and writers.

ISBN: 978-0-9575711-0-5

Written and edited by Alexandra Lockett
Photography by Alexandra Lockett
Archival photographs from various pigeon fanciers

Printed in Belgium by Die Keure
Designed by Keith Dodds

Project Pigeon gratefully acknowledges financial assistance
from the Heritage Lottery Fund.

Supported by
The National Lottery®
through the Heritage Lottery Fund

heritage
lottery fund